Lenses
on Teaching

LENSES ON TEACHING

Developing Perspectives on Classroom Life

Leigh Chiarelott

*Bowling Green
State University*

Leonard Davidman

*California State University
at San Luis Obispo*

Kevin Ryan

Boston University

HOLT, RINEHART AND WINSTON, INC.

Fort Worth   Chicago   San Francisco   Philadelphia   Montreal   Toronto
London   Sydney   Tokyo

Publisher	Ted Buchholz
Acquisitions Editor	Jo-Anne Weaver
Senior Project Editor	Charlie Dierker
Manager of Production	Tad Gaither
Manager of Art & Design	Guy Jacobs
Text Designer	Nancy Sugihara
Cover Designer	Pat Sloan

Cover: HRW photos by Russell Dian

Library of Congress Cataloging-in-Publication Data

Chiarelott, Leigh.
    Lenses on teaching: developing perspectives on classroom life /
Leigh Chiarelott, Leonard Davidman, Kevin Ryan.
      p. cm.
    Includes index.
    1. Observation (Educational method)   2. Teaching. I. Davidman,
Leonard. II. Ryan, Kevin. III. Title.
    LB1027.28.C48 1989
    371.1'02—dc20   89-31903

ISBN: 0-03-013384-X

Address Editorial Correspondence To: 301 Commerce Street, Suite 3700, Fort Worth, TX 76102
Address Orders To: 6277 Sea Harbor Drive, Orlando, FL 32887
1-800-782-4479, or 1-800-433-0001 (in Florida)

Printed in the United States of America

0 1 2 3 066 9 8 7 6 5 4 3 2 1

Holt, Rinehart and Winston, Inc.
The Dryden Press
Saunders College Publishing

Preface

In recent years, national attention has been focused on how best to prepare teachers for the twenty-first century. Both when and how teachers should be educated has been hotly debated by national commissions, teachers' organizations, and teacher-education institutions. One of the common threads among all these proposals for change has been the need for teacher candidates to observe and participate in schools and classrooms early and often during their preparation programs. However, in many of these early field experiences, quantity may not necessarily be equated with quality. To the untrained eye, one classroom practice could appear as effective as another. Having an experience is not, as John Dewey noted, the same as learning from experience. The potential for an experience to be non- or miseducative is increased any time that experience is not accompanied by reflection and analysis.

It was with that thought in mind that *Lenses on Teaching* was created. As a laboratory manual for early, participant, observation-oriented field experiences, it is designed to engage teacher candidates in the experiential triad of action, reflection, and analyses from multiple perspectives and through a variety of conceptual lenses. The activities in this manual, along with the brief essays, journal entries, and questions for discussion are structured around different ways that you can absorb and sort out of the highly complex situations and behaviors you will be observing. From the introductory chapter, which outlines the rationale for and organizational structure of *Lenses on Teaching,* to Chapter 10, which asks you to outline your perceived strengths and weaknesses as a teacher, this manual will engage you in experience that teacher educators have found to be particularly effective in systematically exploring the teaching profession.

We have developed this manual as a guidebook to help you perceive and understand the many things you'll see and do in elementary and secondary classrooms in the next few weeks. You and your instructor may find it useful to do all the activities in the chapters or you may find it necessary to do only the core activity in each chapter. How little or how much you do will be dependent upon your background experience and knowledge and your desire to derive as much benefit as possible from the field experience in which you are placed. In either case, we trust that your experience will be educative.

Although the content of this workbook is ultimately the responsibility of the authors, many persons have contributed in various ways to its successful production. To the many preservice candidates, graduate assistants, and classroom teachers who have shared their conceptual lenses with us and inspired our work through their visions of teaching, we are deeply indebted. To the reviewers whose critiques and insightful suggestions made the text more readable and the activities more workable, we are especially grateful. Among the most notable of these reviewers were: Beverly Jensen, San Jose State University; Ted Cyphert, The Ohio State University; Julia Roncadori, University of Georgia; Dick Clark, University of Massachusetts; Meryl Englander, University of Indiana; Michael V. Belok, Arizona State University; John McIntyre, Southern Illinois University; and Lillian Stephens, State University of New York, Old Westbury.

In addition to those who helped inspire and/or enhance the content of the workbook, we also wish to thank those who contributed to the production of the original manuscript and the final revised draft that ultimately became *Lenses on Teaching*. The Word Processing Center in the College of Education and Allied Professions at Bowling Green State University was an immensely valuable resource in the timely and efficient production of the original draft. Special thanks go to Judy Maxey, Sherry Haskins, and Sheryl Sabo for their excellent work on the original draft. Of course, the final draft would not have been possible without the outstanding efforts of the editorial and production staff at Holt, Rinehart and Winston, and we appreciate their support and expertise in making our vision a reality.

Finally, we are eternally grateful to our families and especially our wives; Donna Chiarelott, whose exceptional indexing skills were invaluable; Pat Davidman, who contributed both style and substance to the content of the workbook; and Marilyn Ryan, who served as a constant source of psychological and intellectual inspiration. Without their encouragement and support this project would never have succeeded.

Brief Table of Contents

Contents

CHAPTER 3

What Is an Effective School?   28

CHAPTER 4

Observing Classroom Interaction   42

CHAPTER 6

Images of the Teacher   130

CHAPTER 10

On Becoming a Teacher   215

Index   236

Lenses
on Teaching

Introduction

Many of you are about to embark on a journey back to an environment where you spent a large portion of your childhood and youth. This time, however, you will be asked to look at this environment from a different perspective (or perhaps multiple perspectives) than you did as a child or adolescent. You will be looking at schools from these different perspectives to help you in your decision to become a teacher. Although you may have already made up your mind to become a teacher, you may be less certain about where you would like to teach, what grade level or subject matter you would feel most confident working with, what type of learners you would find most challenging and rewarding to teach, what kind of school philosophy best mirrors your philosophy of teaching, and so on. Part of the purpose of this journey is to enable you to explore these questions fairly early in your teacher-preparation program so you can begin deciding not only to become a teacher but to reveal to yourself what kind of teacher you would like to become. Ultimately, you will discover that there is much more to teaching than just teaching.

Over the past 15 years, research on effective teaching, classroom management, and the role of field experience in preparing teachers has burgeoned. A recent review of the literature identified over 2,100 articles on effective teaching between 1970 and 1987. On the whole, this research supports the existence of effective teaching and classroom management techniques and has placed field experiences in a pivotal position in the attainment of these competencies.

Early in your field observations you will no doubt feel compelled to note useful techniques employed by the cooperating teacher. Somewhat unconsciously, you will find yourself drawn to behaviors that seem to quiet the students, encourage them to work, motivate interesting discussions, and even make them laugh. These "tricks," as they may seem to you, have an almost mystical effect in the hands of an artistic teacher and there will be a natural tendency to try to mirror those behaviors. Unfortunately, less than effective teachers often have "tricks" as well and these may, at times, seem equally effective in terms of creating quiet, encouragement, motivation, and even enjoyment. Differentiating between the deep structure of classroom life and cosmetic changes brought on by "trickery" will be one of the major dilemmas facing you as you engage in field experiences. Knowing what are essential elements in field observations is a sign of developing maturity in the beginning teacher.

In this resource manual, you will, in a structured, progressive manner, develop skills and knowledge that will enable you to be an insightful, effective observer of classrooms. You will learn to identify and analyze characteristics of schools, classrooms, and learners. You will identify teacher behaviors, effective and ineffective, in a systematic, objective manner. You will utilize instruments for observation that will introduce you to a language for describing classrooms. You will discover recurrent metaphors for schools and schooling and create an "ideal" classroom. You will use strategies to move beyond objective, fragmented descriptions into impressionistic, vivid, and rich descriptions. All of these activities, through diverse means, will contribute to your development as a teacher.

To help you gain the skills of seeing clearly what is going on in schools and classrooms, you will complete a number of tasks. Each task is derived from a key question. Embedded in the questions are the major objectives to be attained in your field-based observations. Through a series of sequentially organized activities, you will see and understand much more of what is going on around you.

Central Questions

The information in this chapter will provide you with an overview of the text as well as an understanding of the activities we are recommending you carry out in the field experience component of your teacher-education program. With this in mind, we have posed some central questions that have shaped the content and form of this resource text. These questions and our responses to them will provide a level of understanding that will enable you to use this resource text more effectively.

Question 1: When should students engage in field observations?

In the recent past, there has been a dramatic change in the way teachers are prepared in the United States. Until a few years ago, most undergraduates, preparing to be teachers, took all of their general education and professional education courses on the campus, until their senior year when they went out to student teach in an elementary or secondary school. There were many problems with that approach. First, most students had to wait four years to discover that, while they liked certain things about education and the teaching career, they were not suited for it. Second, the courses tended to be abstract and remote from the world of children and chalkboards. Third, the teachers-in-training had only their own experience as students to build on. This became troubling when they student taught in kinds of schools different from those they had experienced.

In recent years, teacher-training institutions all over the country have switched to more field-oriented programs. Future teachers are sent into the field during their preparation. The course for which you are using this text is part of this new movement to give greater relevance to your training. Given this shift in perspective regarding the role of field experiences in teacher preparation, most teacher-preparation programs firmly believe that teacher candidates should participate in meaningful, systematic observations early in their teacher-education programs.

Question 2: How should these experiences be organized to ensure meaningful observations?

A sequentially organized and varied set of field experiences should be a key component to this introductory course. The total teaching profession today—teachers, administrators, professors—believe that much of the content that you need to learn exists *within* schools and *within* classrooms. Initially, you will observe the classroom and school using measurement devices that will require you to record information. These instruments will ask you to pay close attention to classroom behaviors and to track them for short periods of time utilizing specially designed coding systems. These instruments will *not* ask you to make judgments or to relate your knowledge and experiences about schools and schooling to the observations you make. Later, as you become more familiar with descriptive ways of looking at classrooms, you will be asked to draw more inferences (i.e., make judgments) about what you are observing. Ultimately, you will be creating your "ideal vision" of classroom teaching as you see it and understand it.

Question 3: Besides observing classroom behaviors, what might be some other valuable resources from which to gather information?

As you become more adept at participant observation and more comfortable in your role as a describer of culture, you'll find that your perspectives are rather limited due to the narrow band of activities you can observe and record. A technique that is particularly helpful in getting us to see more and with greater depth is the skill of interviewing. Although interviewing is a more complex and delicate skill than observing, once you can separate out useful from inappropriate informants, the range of information opened up through interviewing will be of immeasurable value. Among the informants you will interview are students, teachers, administrators, parents of students, and members of the community served by the school. Among the settings in which to conduct an interview will be the classroom, teachers' lounge, school cafeteria, playground, school offices, school-board meetings, places of business in the community, and, perhaps, even the students' homes. No doubt, you will find these various perspectives on schools, schooling, teachers, and teaching illuminating, although sometimes discouraging.

Question 4: How will these activities in observing and interviewing be guided?

Early activities will have specific instructional objectives. By successfully completing the activity, you will have attained the intended outcome of the learning experience. Subsequent experiences will be equally well defined, but the outcomes may be oriented toward problem solving or discovery. One of the major purposes of these activities is to make you increasingly more reliant on your own judgments so that you will begin to see yourself as an effective decision maker.

Question 5: How much of this understanding of schools and teaching will involve self-analysis activities?

Prospective teachers in an introductory, field-based course should engage in self-analysis activities throughout the course so as to be able to discern and describe the change in their educational assumptions, the growth of their educational philosophy, and their personal desires and commitments toward teaching. Inasmuch as artistry involves the projection of one's *self* onto or into a medium, artistic teaching is similarly a projection of one's *self* onto or into a classroom. Artists frequently draw on their past experiences and use perceptions of these experiences as dominant themes in their art. As a teacher, you will need to envision and clarify with yourself and others your experiences in learning and teaching and determine how that affects your perception of teaching. Teaching style is, by and large, an extension of the teacher's personality—his or her expectations, goals, values, attitudes, dreams, idiosyncrasies, and so on. In an effort to comprehend your emerging teaching style, you must, of necessity, come to grips with your *self*. An important part of teacher education is the recognition that you don't suddenly become a teacher at the conclusion of four or five years of preparation. You are becoming, and will continue to become, a teacher for much of your teaching career.

Question 6: In what ways might this continuous growth be fostered?

Because of our firm belief in the growth process of teachers, a series of activities are included in the final chapter of this resource text. These self-education materials are designed to expand upon the observation and interviewing techniques you've acquired and to supplement the self-analysis activities in which you've engaged.

This conception of continuous growth and the activities that support it is predicated upon the assumption that American schools have a critical need for *good* teachers. While the much-discussed teacher shortage (especially in math and science) has captured national attention, it is reminiscent of a similar problem faced in the 1960s. Unfortunately, at that time, the emphasis was placed on educating *more* teachers to meet critical needs, and the research on effective teaching had not yet progressed to the point where it could inform the burgeoning teacher-education programs on the need for continuous-growth experiences. At present, we are in a much stronger position to design activities that enable the development of effective teachers on a continuing basis.

Question 7: **What ideas and facts about teaching and learning inform our vision of effective teaching and the selection of meaningful activities for individuals seeking to become teachers?**

In the past, we have been narrow in our view of learning and teaching. Information was presented and those who retained it were said to have learned. The band of human behaviors that was considered teaching was narrow (lectures and examinations on what was spoken). So, too, was the conception of learning (the echoing of correct answers).

In recent years, the concepts of teaching and learning have been greatly broadened. Now there are many systems or models of teaching, each with specific strengths and limitations. Also, our concept of what constitutes learning has been deepened to take in a wide range of intellectual, physical, emotional, and social changes.

Our vision of good teaching, therefore, has a lot to do with the kind of knowledge teachers draw upon as they make the day-to-day, minute-by-minute decisions that cumulatively provide the foundation upon which good teaching is built. In our view, the knowledge shaping these decisions will derive from: the individual learners themselves; the culture in which the learning and teaching takes place; the body of knowledge about effective teaching in effectively organized schools; and the teacher's own knowledge of curriculum, pedagogy, and self. Several facts are pertinent here.

To begin with, there is the fact that the act of teaching and learning, particularly as it occurs in organizational settings (such as schools, corporations, etc.), is a *culturally* defined and influenced phenomenon. Schools are human creations like fire departments, symphony orchestras, and professional basketball teams. People put them together in a certain way to do a particular job. Therefore, in order to be insightful and effective as a teacher, future teachers must not only know about themselves, they must also know about the culture they live and work in since the culture determines so much of how schools are made. They should be aware of that culture's *subtle* influences on their ways of seeing, feeling, and thinking, and the culture's *powerful* influence on the schools they will most likely teach in.

There is also the fact that, despite organizational patterns that place one teacher in charge of 30 to 40 learners (in our culture) for a day or an hour, teaching and learning is an event, or process, that occurs among *individuals*. Most significantly, these individuals possess learning and teaching styles—

patterns of behavior that stem from their individual preferences, needs, and proclivities—which influence the quality of the learning/teaching event. For instance, some students need to see instructions written out while others need to hear them. These two facts, the cultural fact and the individual fact, combine to produce a major element in our vision of good teaching. For the authors, good teaching will ultimately and inevitably be the kind of teaching that occurs when teachers' instructional and curricular decisions are informed by learning style characteristics of students, as well as an understanding of the cultural and political dimensions of teaching and learning. Because of the significance and complexity of these factors, culture and learning style, individuals seeking to become teachers for and in contemporary educational organizations must commit themselves to becoming persistent, vigorous, proactive learners. Good teaching is created by energetic learners who are constantly bringing new knowledge to bear on their most recent teaching style.

But, as indicated, there are other facts to be considered when one begins to describe a vision of good teaching. Most prominently, there exists today a growing body of recommendations and generalizations about good teaching that emanates from the effective-teaching and effective-school literature. However, this is a double-edged literature with which all future teachers, as well as in-service teachers and administrators, must come to grips. It is a literature that attempts to define *the reality* of good teaching by specifying all those things a teacher will need to be able to do (competencies) before he or she can be certified to be an effective, good, competent, or hireable teacher. These competencies vary from state to state and region to region, but there is an overlap, and our vision of good teaching incorporates this overlap. We believe that when you see good teaching occur in schools across the land, you will be observing a teacher who possesses one transcendent skill, namely, the ability to synthesize cultural, technical, scientific, curricular, instructional, and self-knowledge to create artistic teaching. The activities delineated in this resource text will attempt to put you in touch with educators who are utilizing this skill.

Question 8: What should you know about schooling and education in contemporary America and the world before you embark on your observation and interviewing in selected schools and school districts?

First, you should realize that your perception of what goes on in school is, in effect, the captive of your past experience. Having spent so much time in classrooms as a student makes it difficult to see teaching and learning accurately. If you were to go off and observe how some exotic tribe raises its young or look back historically at a nineteenth-century British preparatory school, you would bring to the task much fresher and less tainted eyes. Realize that you are a prisoner of your own particular school experiences and that they will be in the way of your ability to see things accurately. Finally, you must recognize that the reality you perceive, and the feelings and thoughts these perceptions produce, are culturally bound and culturally determined. If you were to walk into a counseling session between a school psychologist, student, and parent, and the school psychologist was proceeding to do acupuncture on the student, you would probably be surprised and might not realize what was taking place because your culture and your own school experience had not prepared you to see acupuncture in American schools.

Second, you should realize that schools are a social invention and schools, as we know them, are relatively recent in origin. As a social invention, they are one way to solve a social problem, that is, how to introduce the young into productive adult life. As a social invention, they can be replaced, or modified, or ignored. The essential point is that schools have been made by people, and they can be changed by people. As long as people (the taxpayers who pay the bill for schools) are happy, schools will remain the same. When people are unhappy with what happens in schools, things will change as long as the schools exist in a responsive democracy. With this point in mind, as you observe in schools, you should try to discover how the teachers in selected schools try to keep the public happy, and what the consequences are for students.

Third, and related to the issue above, what is taught in school is a community (not federal government or teachers' union) wager concerning what its children will need to know to live well in the twenty-first century. Different communities with different social, ethnic, and economic classes make different wagers. Also, some communities guess better than others and, as a result, their children are much better prepared to meet the future.

Fourth, schools are complex social-political units in which many people and selected organizations play important roles. Some of them are seen (such as teachers, administrators, and janitors) and some are not seen (local school boards, banks, publishers, employers, advertisers, state boards of education and key legislators, labor unions such as the National Education Association, and the district superintendent).

All of these units interact to produce the educational reality you see as well as the educational reality teachers feel, that is, the morale of a school. When you collect your observational data, you should appreciate that you are skimming off the surface of a multilayered, multidimensional organizational network. Indeed, it is as if you were trying to learn about the human body by focusing attention on the eyes, ears, legs, arms, skin, nose, and mouth. These surface features are all fascinating and do inform you about the human body, but they do not constitute the entire being. As you look in individual classrooms to learn about the role of teachers, keep this multidimensional complexity in mind.

Fifth, classrooms are ideas in action. Usually, behind any planned classroom activity is a set of ideas about what a person is, how they learn, what they need to learn, what each child's relationship with others should be, and what are worthy purposes of living. These ideas are not clearly visible on the surface of the classroom, but are embedded in what is learned and how the teacher organizes what he or she does. Even if the teacher is not conscious of these ideas in action, they are having an effect.

The central questions above may trigger a number of questions in your mind. To begin with, you may wonder why we believe it is so important that potential teacher candidates engage in the field activities contained in this text so early in the teacher-preparation program.

The answer concerns attitudes. Research, as well as the authors' own experience, suggests that a large percentage of prospective teachers have unusually romantic, unrealistic notions of what teaching in the modern classroom is all about. For such candidates, exposure to the professional educators in their workplace becomes a form of career counseling; students get an early chance to examine their assumptions about teaching. In addition to the examination of assumptions, there are the important research skills of observing and interviewing that prospective teachers will draw on during student teaching and throughout their careers in teaching. Because of the usefulness and importance of these skills, prospective teachers need to learn how to observe and interview professionally as soon as possible.

At this point, you may be ready to ask: *When* do classroom teachers in general employ these observation and interviewing skills? The answer is that good teachers observe their students all the time in a number of important areas to help make a number of important decisions. They initially observe patterns of verbal and nonverbal behavior and a student's leadership in small and large groups. They analyze interactions between child and child, and child and adults. They pick up on unusual reading behaviors (such as eye strain), listening behaviors (such as straining to hear), children's emotional state, physical health, and so on. At the same time, they also learn about the students by interviewing them as well as their parents and former teachers.

The emphasis on interviewing may surprise you somewhat since interviewing is not, typically, thought of as a teaching task. In fact, however, good teachers need to be good interviewers. Ted Wheeler, an experienced elementary-school teacher in San Luis Obispo, California, really believes in interviewing. He regularly conducts a 20- to 30-minute interview with the parents or guardian of each of his students during the first five weeks of school. During this most important first encounter with parents, he asks questions such as:

1. Tell me a little bit about your child.
2. What responsibilities does your child have at home?
3. What do you do if your child doesn't obey the family rules? Does it work?
4. What are some things you'd like your child to learn in our class this year?
5. Is your child on any type of medication?
6. Would you be interested in helping the class (or school) as a volunteer?

This type of first-conference interview will: begin to open up trust between parent(s) and teacher; provide you with up-to-date health and family information (phone number, address, etc.); get more parents involved in public schooling; and will set the stage for later three-way conferences between student, parent(s), and the teacher. Teachers will also utilize in-depth interviews with: students who enter the class later in the year after the teacher has gone through a good deal of diagnostic activity with students at the beginning of the year, and other experienced teachers.

Another teacher, Paula McGrath from Dedham, Massachusetts, considers herself a "skilled child watcher." When she meets a new class each fall, she makes a special effort to observe how each child behaves and to observe each child in many different settings such as the playground, in reading groups, or working alone. She records as much of what she sees as possible in anecdotal records for each child, records that she goes back to think about and analyze when problems arise.

Ted Wheeler and Paula McGrath are part of a new wave of teachers who are putting together some old and some new skills to make themselves outstanding teachers. It is our intention to introduce you to and provide you practice with this blend of old and new skills. Unlike these teachers who have had to develop most of these skills on their own in unstructured situations with little or no feedback on their rates of success, you will be given considerable guidance throughout. With this in mind, you should be ready to take the first step in developing your skills as a participant-observer.

A *User's Guide to* Lenses on Teaching

We have structured this workbook to make your field experiences as educative as possible. From the central questions we've posed, you've probably concluded that you will be developing many new skills, acquiring much useful information, and examining a variety of emerging and existing attitudes and values. To accomplish this, we have structured each of the chapters around a similar format that will facilitate your observations and maximize your attainment of the course objectives.

Although the chapters are sequenced in a manner that reflects both the chronology of your field experiences and the intensity in which you will engage in them, it may be convenient to modify the sequence to match more coherently the structure of your unique field experience. In general, the workbook can be resequenced to utilize the unique qualities of your field experience to best advantage.

Each chapter has four parts. The first part of each chapter is a brief essay that will introduce you to the phenomena that should be observed or discovered during that particular visit to the school. The essay will also introduce you to the activities that constitute the "meat" of the chapter. In some cases, the activities, which make up the second part of the chapter, are interspersed with the essay portion and at other times they stand on their own. The activities are either labeled as "Core" activities or "Suggested" activities. The Core Activities are central to the field experience and should be completed by everyone, while the Suggested Activities can be utilized either in part or in their entirety. The Suggested Activities can be used to augment the Core Activity, to provide enrichment activities for individuals or small groups of students, or to facilitate the assignment of individual group tasks for large classes.

The third part of the chapter is the journal entry that asks you to reflect upon the observation you've just made and to record your feelings about the phenomena you've observed. These entries should consist of your private thoughts, emerging feelings, new insights, and inner struggles regarding teaching as a career. The journal should be a communication device between you and your instructor and should only be shared between the two of you. You should find the journal entry to be a useful device for self-exploration.

The final part of the chapter consists of a series of questions for discussion. These questions revolve around issues brought up in the essay portion of the chapter and deal with insights you should have gained from the observations and activities you completed during that week's field experience. These questions can be responded to orally or in writing or both and can also be assigned to specific teams within the class. They provide an important closure activity for that set of observations.

Eventually, this part of your journey toward becoming a teacher will end. We hope this workbook will provide you with considerable guidance as you complete the journey and ultimately understand your reasons for becoming or not becoming a teacher. The lenses you acquire as you make this journey will provide you with new ways to look at schools, classrooms, teachers, students, and, in the end, yourself.

References

Gearing, F., & Hughes, W. (1975). *On observing well: Self-instruction in ethnographic observation for teachers, principals, and supervisors.* Amhurst, N.Y.: Center for Studies of Cultural Transmission, State University of New York at Buffalo.

Henry, M. A. (1983, Spring/Summer). The effect of increased exploratory field experiences upon the perceptions and performance of student teachers. *Action in Teacher Education, 5,* 66–70.

Jackson, P. (1968). *Life in classrooms.* New York: Holt, Rinehart and Winston.

Popkewitz, T. (1977). Ideology as a problem of teacher education. Paper presented at the Annual Meeting of the American Educational Research Association, New York.

Spradley, J. P., & McCurdy, D. W. (eds.). (1972). *The cultural experience: Ethnography in complex society.* Chicago, Ill.: Science Research Associates.

CHAPTER 2

Orienting Yourself to Schools

Over the next few weeks you will engage in some intensive observations in local elementary, junior high/middle schools, and/or high schools. These schools may be located in inner-city, urban areas, suburban areas, or rural areas. Some schools may remind you of your own school experiences while others will be new to you. Throughout your observations in these schools, you will be sorting out your own feelings about teachers, students, administrators, schools, and ultimately about your decision to become a teacher. In this chapter, we will provide activities that will orient you to the situation you're observing and enable you to derive more meaningful information from subsequent observations.

You may wonder why you are being asked to spend so much time in schools as part of your teacher-preparation program. After all, you've already spent over 16,000 hours in school before you came to college. If quantity of time in classrooms, in and of itself, were sufficient preparation for career decision making, then these initial observations would be superfluous. Yet, research has consistently shown that early field experiences are essential to both career decision making and to the development of teaching skills in the areas of instruction and classroom management (Lanier & Little, 1987).

Teachers firmly believe that field experiences were critical to their preparation program and frequently bemoan the fact that there aren't more and better experiences before student teaching (Lanier & Little, 1987). What is at issue is how to derive the greatest possible benefit from these field experiences in terms of helping you decide whether to become a teacher, and in helping you discover the kind of teacher you want to become. By encountering teaching and learning in a variety of contexts and under a wide range of conditions, you will catch glimpses of yourself as a teacher with an emerging teaching style. With the activities in this chapter and in subsequent chapters, these glimpses will slowly blend into a tapestry whose pattern will become increasingly clear to you as you reflect on your own experiences and those of others. Eventually you will feel comfortable in characterizing yourself as a teacher, and in taking your first steps toward self-direction in your career choice and self-development.

The first step in this orientation process involves actually visiting and spending considerable time in a local school(s). Depending upon your school experience, your reaction to this proposition probably ranges somewhere between thrilling and chilling. Your mind will no doubt conjure up images of children happily engaged in activities at work stations, excited buzzing in the hallways, lively discussions in the classroom, and curious learners asking who you are and what you're doing there. You may also visualize faces of kids unlike those you went to school with, little "rug rats" grabbing you around the leg or throwing up on your shoes, food fights, and the odors that unmistakably tell you that you're "in school."

A myriad of questions run through your mind: What should I wear? How should I act? Will I really be teaching or will I only be running dittos? Whom should I talk to and about what? What will I do with my time? Do I have to eat lunch there? Will the kids accept me or will they think I'm a jerk? Don't feel that you're alone in asking these questions. Everyone feels some trepidation when encountering a new experience and you're no different. What is different is that while you've been in schools before, you haven't looked at them from the perspective of the teacher. It may take you a while to feel comfortable in that role, and the transition may not be easy. The following activities will help you in making that transition.

Suggested Activity One

Arriving at the School

Upon your arrival at school, someone in authority should greet you and provide background information on the school itself, the expectations the school's staff has for you, the kinds of experiences you might expect to have at the school, and some basic ground rules that will make your stay at the school more pleasant. Generally, the person who greets you will be the building principal or assistant principal, although this task is sometimes turned over to others knowledgeable about the school such as a guidance counselor or head teacher. To gain the most information about the school during this orientation, your group may want to ask some of the following questions:

Orientation Questions

1. How many students attend the school and what is the approximate average class size?
2. How long are class periods (if a high school or junior high)? How much time do teachers spend on reading, math, science, and social studies (if an elementary school)?
3. Do teachers and students have any free periods (or recess)?

4. What special duties must teachers perform each day or on a regular basis?

5. In your opinion, what makes this school particularly pleasant to work in?

6. Are there special rules or policies that help make the school run smoothly?

7. Are there particular activities or achievements for which the school is well known in the area?

8. Has the school building or the school environment undergone any noteworthy changes or improvements recently?

9. How diverse is the student population? Does that present any special challenges to the staff?

10. Are there any areas or activities that you would especially like us to observe while we're in your school?

After your introduction to the school, you may find that you've formed strong initial impressions of it. Based upon the sights, sounds, and smells that you've encountered, you're probably sensing or feeling a "comfort level" upon which you'll be able to operate in this building. What you are experiencing are sensations that are telling you areas you want to visit, areas you want to avoid, people you want to find out more about, students you want to observe more extensively, and so on. These initial impressions will have a significant impact upon your first few observations and, to some extent, will "frame" that experience by providing a context within which to interpret the experiences you're having.

For that reason, it is important for you to elicit your initial impressions of the school and to write them down for closer examination. The process of writing them down will help you to understand the feelings you're having about schools and about teaching. They will also provide a useful point of reference to return to after you've completed *all* your observations. You may be surprised to discover how your feelings have varied from the beginning of your observations to the end.

Suggested Activity Two
Initial Impressions of School Building

For this activity, you should use the sheet on the next page to record your initial impressions of the school. Many of your statements will resemble a "free association" as you link a sensation with an impression. That's a logical way to talk to yourself as you're walking around the building or listening to an orientation session. It is important that you move from those impressions based upon sensations to a set of conclusions based upon your impressions. As soon as possible after you've completed Part One of this activity, try to complete Part Two.

Part One: My Initial Impressions of the School

1. _____

_____

2. _____

_____

3. _____

_____

4. _____

_____

5. _____

_____

6. _____

_____

7. _____

_____

8. _____

_____

9. _____

_____

10. _____

_____

Part Two: What Do My Impressions Lead Me to Conclude about the School?

1. Conclusions about the building: _____

   _____

   _____

   _____

2. Conclusions about the administration: _____

   _____

   _____

   _____

3. Conclusions about the teachers: _____

   _____

   _____

   _____

4. Conclusions about the students: _____

   _____

   _____

   _____

5. Conclusions about the community: _____

   _____

   _____

   _____

Now that you have some fairly well-formed conclusions about the nature of the school building and how it operates, try to respond to specific questions about the school as though you were being interviewed by someone who had never visited this school before. Be as vivid and descriptive as possible in your responses.

Suggested Activity Three*
Describing the School

---

1. Describe the physical characteristics of this school. Is the building old or new? What are the exterior and the grounds like? Does the building appear inviting? How is it decorated inside? Are certain areas carpeted? What impression do you get from these physical facilities?

2. From what you observed, can you tell who is in charge? What incidents have you observed that suggest that some individuals have control over others?

3. How do people dress in this school? Are there differences among the various groups of people?

---

*(Ryan, Burkholder, & Phillips, 1983)

4. Is there a central or official place where authority resides? What are some things you observed that led to your conclusion?

5. Are some places more physically comfortable? Who gets to use them?

6. How are the students working? What are they doing? Are they working singly or in groups? Are they quiet? Or are they talking freely?

7. Is there a special area for public displays? If so, what is in them and what do they say about this school? Go into the teachers' lounge(s) and places where they eat and observe the physical facilities, the information on the bulletin boards, and the behavior of individuals and if and how that behavior differs from "public" behavior. What are some of the topics that people talk about?

8. Finally, report anything that happened to you in the process of making the observation. These include encounters with people or questions about what you were doing. Also, comment on things you expected to happen that did not. Conclude by giving your general impressions of the school that you visited.

While school buildings tend to be similar, classrooms are diverse in the way they are arranged, decorated, and used. Classrooms appear to have a personality and that personality is a curious blend of the teacher's style and the stu-

Are the classrooms you are observing organized to enhance student learning?

"And then, of course, there's the possibility of being just the slightest bit too organized."

Glen Dines KAPPAN

dents' needs and values. Classrooms offer interesting contrasts in both form and function. Some classrooms appear to be living spaces while others appear to be places where people work. Some are vividly decorated and vibrant in tone while others are stark and uninviting. Although elementary classrooms seem to be more inviting than secondary classrooms, there are secondary classrooms that excite both the senses and the imagination. However, since secondary teachers often move from room to room in their day's teaching, most secondary classrooms lack the fine touches that accumulate in delightful ways in elementary classrooms.

Since the bulk of your observation time will be spent in the classroom, there should be ample opportunity to sketch out a detailed map that depicts where the teacher and students are located as well as unique features of the room's organization. Besides showing the physical layout of the classroom, identify the more subtle features as well. For example, is the room lighted naturally or artificially? Are desks designed for maximum mobility? Does the physical arrangement of the desks facilitate the use of a variety of teaching strategies? Are bulletin boards or displays coordinated with the unit or course content? Are media hardware (i.e., televisions, computers, overhead projectors, screens) located in such a way as to enhance instruction and learning (Emmer, Evertson, Stanford, Clements, & Worsham, 1983)?

Student Name _____   Date _____

Below is a space you can use to diagram the classroom you are observing, as viewed from above. Include as much detail as possible.

Core Activity

Mapping the Classroom

Based on your map, respond to the following questions:

1. In what ways is the organization of the classroom conducive to student learning? In what ways does it inhibit learning?

2. Given this classroom organization, what would you expect to be important elements of the teacher's philosophy or style of teaching?

3. Do the students and the teacher appear to be comfortable with the classroom organization? On what do you base this conclusion?

4. If you were the teacher, how would you modify this classroom to fit your style of teaching?

During this first visit to the school, you've encountered many individuals who made an impression on you. It may have been an administrator who introduced you to the school building and to your cooperating teacher, it may have been the classroom teacher you observed, or it may have been a student (or students) that you were drawn to throughout the observation. It could even have been a person on the school staff such as the office secretary, a maintenance worker, or a cafeteria helper. Over the next few weeks these individuals may have a considerable impact on your decision to become a teacher and it will be useful to think about how these people might affect your perceptions of schools, teaching, and learning.

Based upon this initial contact, try to identify the person who made the most vivid impression on you and analyze why she or he affected you this way. The impression may have been either positive or negative, but the critical element will be to discern how this individual might alter or enhance your perception of a career in teaching. Use the form below to describe, analyze, and evaluate the impression this individual made on you.

Suggested Activity Four
The Most Memorable Person

---

1. Description of the Person Who Made the Most Vivid Impression on Me (include in this description the role this person has in the school, how you interacted with him or her, and a brief discussion of what he or she did to make such a vivid impression on you).

2. Analysis of Why this Person Might Affect Your Perceptions of the School (include in this analysis a description of how this person affected you, in what way he or she altered your perceptions, and why he or she might influence your decision about teaching).

3. Evaluation of the Person Who Impressed You Most Vividly (include in this evaluation your feelings about why this person might influence you, what you've discovered about yourself through interacting with this person, and whether you should allow your perceptions to be influenced by him or her).

Your first observation in the school has left you with a variety of feelings, some vivid impressions, and a tremendous number of questions. Use these feelings, impressions, and questions to generate a list of things you would like to do or see in your remaining observations. The journal entry on the following page is a logical place to include this list as well as to record a few of the reactions you had to your first visit to the school. Because this is your first journal entry, you should complete it as soon as possible after your visit to the school.

Student Name _____   Date _____

Journal Entry

Since this is your first journal entry based upon your first impressions of the school and of the teacher(s) you are observing, use those impressions as the focal point of this entry. Concentrate on the school structure, its functional nature and its aesthetic qualities. How do you feel about the school and the conditions under which teaching and learning occur? What are your initial impressions of the teacher's workload? How could you summarize your feelings about teaching right now?

_____

_____

_____

_____

_____

_____

_____

_____

_____

_____

_____

_____

_____

_____

_____

_____

_____

_____

Questions for Discussion

1. Based on your initial observations, what are your impressions of the school and its role in the education of the community and the teacher and his or her role(s) in the school? Did those impressions change from what they were before your observation? Why?

2. Analyze your impressions of the school. What aspects of the school made the biggest impression on you? Were most of your impressions positive or negative? How might these impressions affect later observations?

3. Analyze the classroom you observed in terms of its physical arrangement. In what ways is the physical arrangement conducive to teaching and learning? In what ways is it detrimental? If this were your classroom, how would you change it?

4. Describe your feelings as you did your walking tour of the school. What impressed you regarding its physical structure, organization, resources, aesthetics, and so on? What did you dislike about it? Did you regard the school as inviting or discouraging learning? In what ways might your impressions change during subsequent observations?

References

Emmer, E. T., Evertson, C. M., Sanford, J. P., Clements, B. S., & Worsham, M. E. (1983). *Organizing and managing the junior high school classroom.* Austin, Tex. The Research and Development Center for Teacher Education (University of Texas at Austin), 6–15.

Lanier, J., & Little, J. (1987). Research on teacher education in *Handbook of research on teaching,* 3rd edition, Merlin C. Wittrock (ed.). New York: Macmillan, 550–552.

Ryan, K., Burkholder, S., & Phillips, D. H. (1983). *The workbook: Exploring careers in teaching.* Columbus, Ohio: Merrill, 49–50.

CHAPTER 3

What Is an Effective School?

During your first observation(s) you were able to collect some strong impressions of the school building, its classrooms, a teacher's workday and, to some extent, the role of the administrator. Chances are that with little effort you synthesized these impressions and concluded that your assigned school was either operating effectively or ineffectively. You based this conclusion largely on how you would like a school to operate and how closely this school's operation matched your ideal. Perhaps you felt that your elementary or high school operated effectively and since this school's operation closely mirrored your school's, it must be effective. These conclusions are generally useful because they help us frame our experiences and provide guidance as to the kind of school settings in which we'd feel comfortable working.

Conclusions, however, are useful only to the extent to which the evidence they're based upon is solid. Initial impressions, though powerful, can be misleading. In this chapter, you will be given a structured observational instrument that will help you collect evidence on school effectiveness. This evidence may support or refute your initial impressions but, more importantly, it will strengthen the evidence upon which you base your conclusions.

Defining Effective Schools

For some time, researchers believed that there was little that schools could do to overcome the effects of a student's home life, social and economic standing, and lack of educative experiences outside the school (Coleman, Campbell, Hobson, McPartland, Mood, Winfield, & York, 1966). These non-school factors were seen as powerful forces that limited the effectiveness of skillful administrators, imaginative curricula, and talented teachers. In schools where resources were scarce, the picture was even bleaker. The expectations for academic achievement in these schools were exceedingly low.

In the mid-1970s a group of researchers (New York State Department of Education, 1974) began to question some of these assumptions because they

28

had observed schools in these so-called deprived areas that were succeeding remarkably well in terms of academic achievement. They wondered what characteristics these "effective schools" shared that made them seem more successful than other schools in the area. They began to search for commonalities, or correlates, among the effective schools. They looked for common elements in the way the schools were administered, what areas of the curriculum were emphasized, how students were instructed and evaluated, and the overall environment of the school building. For the most part, they concentrated their research in urban schools and in elementary schools.

Not surprisingly, researchers found a number of factors that the effective schools had in common, but for our purposes we'll limit the list to the five that appear to have captured the most attention in the literature on effective schools. While educators are far from unanimous in their belief that these factors are the *only* way to determine effective schools (Purkey & Smith, 1983), the factors, or correlates, do provide a set of global indexes by which you can judge the school you're observing. The five correlates are:

1. Strong building leadership
2. High expectations of all students (i.e., mastery of a minimum level of skills by *all*)
3. Orderly, but not rigid, classroom and school atmosphere
4. Acquisition of basic skills takes precedence over all other school activities
5. Frequent monitoring of pupil progress

Some of these correlates appear to be supportable on the basis of common sense, but others are controversial. You may find yourself strongly disagreeing with several of the following assertions, but keep in mind that the correlates and the specific practices that flow from them are having a profound effect on some schools. You may judge for yourself just how well they would have worked in your school.

CORRELATE ONE: STRONG BUILDING LEADERSHIP

In the schools that were judged to be effective, the building principals exhibited considerable influence on the quality of teaching and teachers, the school environment, and the academic lives of the students. The school staff frequently labeled these principals as "instructional leaders." Most of their energy was directed toward making the schools into places where high-quality learning could take place.

Principals of effective schools work tirelessly to make instruction their number-one priority. Resources are devoted to enhancing instructional materials, encouraging teachers to employ research-based teaching techniques, creating classes of manageable size, and using teacher aides and resource persons. These principals know exactly what is going on in the school and are exceedingly proud of their teachers, students, and programs and don't hesitate to share that information by frequently inviting people into the building. The principal and the school have a clear sense of mission and that is evident in the way the school is run.

Based on your observations, is the principal a strong, positive influence on the school?

"We don't have a leader here, just our principal, Mr. Langburn."

originally published in Phi Delta Kappan

CORRELATE TWO: HIGH EXPECTATIONS

One of the basic tenets of learning is that people tend to rise (or fall) to the level of expectation conveyed to them. This "self-fulfilling prophecy" has been well documented (Rosenthal & Jacobson, 1968), and its effects are pervasive. In many schools, teachers have reached the point of negotiating student behavior (Sizer, 1984). They don't push the students too hard and, in return, the students maintain a modicum of decorum in the classroom. Teachers don't assign homework because they know students won't do it anyway. Students in lower math groups or curricular "tracks" are not challenged because they just can't handle the work. Their classwork is usually mundane and task oriented because they would just misbehave if they were given creative or out-of-the-ordinary assignments to do. In short, a vicious circle emerges that conveys the following: lower expectations yield lower levels of performance that reinforce lower expectations.

In effective schools, the opposite is true. Students receive the message early on that high levels of performance are expected and rewarded. Teachers are expected to plan their lessons extensively and to provide well-organized, academically substantial content. Homework is assigned when appropriate (and it is frequently appropriate!), and it is graded and returned to the student. Some schools even have well-articulated homework policies. The emphasis is on academic achievement and this achievement is rewarded. Students may receive academic achievement "letters" and letter sweaters, much like athletes. Teachers are expected to keep up in their fields and incentives are provided for improving teaching skills. Mastery learning rather than competitive, norm-referenced grading is encouraged. Finally, there is a strong emphasis on attaining performance goals. Teachers frequently post on bulletin boards or on classroom walls the learning objectives students have attained and those that will be attained in the future. The emphasis is on what students *can* do and not what they can't do.

CORRELATE THREE: ORDERLY, BUT NOT RIGID, LEARNING ENVIRONMENT

As might be expected, effective schools stressed orderliness and control but not to the point of repression. While effective schools could hardly be called bastions of individual freedom, there was a feeling of personal liberty that arose from being in a relatively safe environment. This was achieved through the establishment of a kind of "social contract" in the school building. Students were expected to behave appropriately and were rewarded for doing so. Rules were created but kept to a minimum and the emphasis tended to be more on responsibilities than rules. Most importantly, teachers were expected to teach and students to learn and any activities that interrupted that goal were either eliminated or kept to a minimum.

These effective schools were characterized by the positive learning climate that existed in the classrooms, hallways, study halls, lunch rooms, and so on. This climate was not attained by enforcing the educational equivalent of martial law but was achieved by directing student energies toward attainable learning outcomes and promoting a sense of ownership within the school buildings. The school grounds and physical plant were well kept and there were almost no signs of vandalism or wholesale destruction of property.

Instructionally, classes tended to be run in a businesslike manner with crisp, well-defined activities clearly in evidence. Classes began promptly and little time was wasted with false starts, weak transitions between activities, or aimless meanderings toward an ill-conceived goal. There were few interruptions by P.A. announcements, pull-out programs, or unplanned visits from the office. In short, the classroom, like the school building, emphasized the maximization of opportunities for learning.

CORRELATE FOUR: SKILLS ACQUISITION TAKES PRECEDENCE OVER ALL OTHER ACTIVITIES

The fourth correlate is probably the most controversial of the five. It is linked to both the creation of positive learning climates and high expectations, but it has been strongly criticized for its narrowness of curricular scope and its naïveté regarding why students come to school in the first place. In essence, it squares off basic skills with extracurricular activities. It takes the position that in too many noneffective schools the extracurricular tail is wagging the curricular dog.

In effective schools, it is believed that students who attend school should be *guaranteed* minimum competence in reading, writing, and computation and that no one should leave school functionally illiterate. To attain this goal, the entire curriculum for some students could be focused on skills. Secondary students would be ineligible for or severely limited in their participation in extracurricular activities until basic skills were acquired. Elementary students would have much of their curricular days apportioned to reading, language arts, and mathematics with other areas kept to state-department minimums. In some cases, arts or expressive curricular areas would be noticeably reduced until the basics were covered. Needless to say, this attack on extracurricular activities and expressive curricular outcomes was not well received by critics who argued that these activities made school palatable for a great many students, and that these activities—art, music, and physical education in particular—were critical areas of human intelligence *and* well-being.

A focal point for observing this correlate in schools should be the manner in which the administrator and ultimately the teachers have chosen to emphasize basics. How much time is apportioned in the elementary buildings to the acquisition of basic skills and how are these skills defined? How are students remediated at the secondary level and are reading and writing stressed across the curriculum? What role do expressive arts (drama, music, art, dance, etc.) play in the curriculum and how are extracurricular activities handled during the school day? Are students pulled out of class for band practice, choir rehearsal, track meets, football or basketball games, and so on? How do teachers and students feel about the emphasis on basic skills? Because of the controversial nature of this correlate, you may find these observations and responses rather enlightening and informative.

CORRELATE FIVE: FREQUENT MONITORING OF PUPIL PROGRESS

Perhaps the least controversial of the correlates, the frequent monitoring of pupil progress, is firmly grounded in learning theory and pedagogical practice. Since the early 1900s, feedback has been a component of one of the basic principles of learning. It has been argued that learning cannot proceed in the absence of feedback. A learner must be regularly apprised of how well he or she is performing in order to be successful at attaining learning outcomes.

In effective schools, considerable time and energy is spent early in the academic year collecting data on student achievement and ability. These preassessments are integral to planning instruction and setting attainable learning outcomes for students. In programs where mastery learning approaches are utilized, the preassessment data are essential for student placement. They are also critical in situations where students are grouped by ability, developmentally or by learning style preferences.

When students receive feedback frequently and promptly, the feedback itself becomes more meaningful. This means that teachers return written work promptly and with specific reinforcing remarks or corrective cues. When students make computational or grammatical errors, for example, they are shown specifically what the error is and how to correct it. Because students are constantly receiving evaluative information, their grades are rarely a surprise and therefore not threatening. Generally, the teacher employs a variety of evaluative methods and incorporates these into most lessons on a daily basis. By monitoring student progress frequently, teachers can communicate in a more informed manner with both the student and his or her parent(s).

Using the Five Correlates in Your Observations

As we indicated earlier, the effective-schools model has been criticized because it doesn't provide explicit guidelines for making schools more effective nor does it provide a set of research-based characteristics that are uniformly agreed upon. These criticisms notwithstanding, there is much in the five correlates we described above to explain why some schools are operating more effectively than others. What these correlates do provide is a basis for looking at schools in a systematic way. Because of the information you gather by using the instrument on the following pages, you can create your own image of an effective school in a more informed manner. As a result, you may add to or delete from the characteristics presented and draw different conclusions as to what constitutes an effective school.

Core Activity
Collecting Information

On the following pages you will collect information on the school you're assigned to and draw some conclusions as to the overall effectiveness of the school. Some of your information will come from observations and some will come from asking specific questions of teachers and students. Keep in mind that you are only collecting information at this stage and not drawing conclusions. Conclusions should be reached after you have thoroughly analyzed the information you've collected and compared your analysis with those of your classmates or observational team.

If you are organized into teams, it is recommended that each team be comprised of five members and that each member be assigned a different correlate. After each member has completed his or her data collection, all the data should be compiled into a final report including a set of conclusions.

Because this activity requires considerable data collection over a period of time, you should consider it to be an ongoing activity covering several visits to the school. It will be useful to compare notes frequently with your teammates to ensure consistency in your data-gathering methods. This consistency will be particularly important when it comes time to write your conclusions.

Directions for Collecting Data

To use the instrument on the following pages to determine the effectiveness of the school you're observing in, you will need to make some observations and respond to questions related to these observations. To elaborate on your impressions, you may need to ask students, teachers, or administrators a few brief questions, but do this only to gain information, not to challenge their perceptions. Primarily, you should try to strengthen your skills through careful and attentive observation.

Student Name _____ Date _____

Effective School Correlate	A Questions	B Observations
Instructional leadership	Respond to the following questions briefly to elaborate on your observations in column B.	Indicate by marking "yes" or "no" whether you observed the following activities.
	What does the principal do?	The principal of the building is often seen around the building. _____ Yes _____ No
	What is the principal's function	The principal relates well with the students and the teachers. _____ Yes _____ No
	How do the principal and the teachers work together in the school?	The principal is proud of the school and communicated that to you. _____ Yes _____ No
	How does the principal interact with the students	The principal appears to play an important role in making the school work effectively and efficiently. _____ Yes _____ No
High expectations for students and staff	How often are students expected to do homework?	There is a clearly articulated homework policy. _____ Yes _____ No
	Are unit plans and lesson plans developed and reviewed by administrators?	Unit plans and lesson plans are readily accessible and/or visible. _____ Yes _____ No
	Do students appear to be challenged as learners?	
	What incentives are used to encourage student achievement?	There is evidence of tangible rewards for academic excellence. _____ Yes _____ No

Orderly, but not rigid, learning environment

How are teachers rewarded for being exceptionally effective in the classroom?

There are incentives for good teaching.
___ Yes ___ No

Teachers challenge students and/or convey high expectations to them.
___ Yes ___ No

What do you like most about the school?

Did you have a positive feeling about the school as you walked around it?
___ Yes ___ No

Do you feel that the school is well organized?

Did you feel safe?
___ Yes ___ No

Are there interruptions in classes that you find annoying?

Was it well organized?
___ Yes ___ No

Was there evidence of school rules? Are students expected to follow them? How are they enforced?

Are students rewarded for behaving appropriately?
___ Yes ___ No

Do the students get along well with each other and with the teachers?

The classrooms are well organized.
___ Yes ___ No

Do you feel that class sizes are adequate for maintaining order?

A lot of time is wasted in the classrooms.
___ Yes ___ No

Was hallway traffic smooth or chaotic?
___ Smooth ___ Chaotic

Were students in the hallways during classes?
___ Yes ___ No

Were they there for legitimate reasons?
___ Yes ___ No

The appearance of the building and the grounds was attractive.
___ Yes ___ No

Was there evidence of vandalism?
___ Yes ___ No

Did students treat each other's property with respect?
___ Yes ___ No

Are reading and writing emphasized?
___ Yes ___ No

Are math skills emphasized?
___ Yes ___ No

Did extracurricular activities seem to interrupt the learning activities in the school?
___ Yes ___ No

Were extracurricular activities scheduled only after school?
___ Yes ___ No

Did students have opportunities to play or have "free" periods?
___ Yes ___ No

Was there an emphasis on academics and on doing well academically in school?
___ Yes ___ No

Are students graded on a regular basis?
___ Yes ___ No

Emphasis on basic skills

How much class time is allocated for each of the subjects taught in the elementary classroom?

Are reading and writing emphasized in *all* courses in the high school?

Do students appear to have learned to read and write reasonably well? How effective are their math skills? What subjects do students appear to enjoy most in school? Least like?

To what extent are basic skills emphasized in the school?

What role do extracurricular activities play in the school?

What extra activities does the school provide for students?

Monitoring student progress frequently

Are students preassessed and how is that data useful?

Student Name _____   Date _____

How often are students graded by the teachers?

Do students seem to do the homework assigned to them?

How are students evaluated? How is student progress reported to the students and their parent(s)?

How do teachers grade students' daily work? Tests?

Do teachers use a variety of strategies to teach and to evaluate student learning?
_____ Yes _____ No

Do teachers determine if students have learned what was taught at some point in the lesson?
_____ Yes _____ No

Are students grouped for instruction?
_____ Yes _____ No

Does the teacher give feedback to students?
_____ Yes _____ No

Do students react to this feedback?
_____ Yes _____ No

38

Student Name _____   Date _____

Journal Entry

During this observation, you were asked to use an instrument to gather information. In your journal, indicate how you felt about collecting information this way and about the way people responded when you asked them questions. Finally, share some of your thoughts on how we might judge a school's effectiveness and whether the information you gathered made you more aware of how to make these judgments.

_____

_____

_____

_____

_____

_____

_____

_____

_____

_____

_____

_____

_____

_____

_____

_____

_____

_____

Questions for Discussion

1. Is it possible to judge a school's effectiveness on the basis of your observations? What information did you feel was missing and how would you go about gathering that information?

2. Did you agree with the criteria for judging effective schools discussed in this chapter? What criteria would you add or delete?

3. According to the information you and your classmates gathered, how do effective schools differ from ineffective schools? What ways would you suggest to improve the ineffective schools? What problems would you have teaching in a school that you judged to be ineffective?

4. How might you use the observational instrument provided in this chapter to help you in adjusting to the school in which you do your practice teaching? How might it help you select the school in which you take your first teaching job? In judging your children's school as a parent?

References

Brookover, W. B., & Lezotte, L. W. (1979). *Changes in school characteristics coincident with changes in student achievement.* (ERIC Document Reproduction Service No. ED 181 005).

Coleman, J. S., Campbell, E. Q., Hobson, C. J., McPartland, J., Mood, A. M., Winfield, F. D., & York, R. L. (1966). *Equality of educational opportunity.* Washington, D.C.: U.S. Department of Health, Education, and Welfare.

Edmonds, R. R., & Fredericksen, J. R. (1979). *Search for effective schools: The identification and analysis of city schools that are instructionally effective for poor children.* (ERIC Document Reproduction Service No. ED 20 396).

Good, T., & Brophy, J. (1973). *Looking in classrooms.* New York: Harper & Row.

Jencks, C. L., Smith, M., Acland, H., Bane, M. S., Cohen, D. K., Gintis, H., Heyns, B. L., & Michaelson, S. (1972). *Inequality: A reassessment of the effects of family and schooling in America.* New York: Basic Books.

New York State Department of Education. (1974). *School factors influencing reading achievement: A case study of two inner city schools.* Albany, N.Y.: Office of Education Performance Review.

Purkey, S. C., & Smith, M. S. (March, 1983). Effective schools: A review. *The Elementary School Journal, 83,* (4), 427–452.

Rosenthal, R., & Jacobson, L. (1968). *Pygmalion in the classroom: Teacher expectation and pupils' intellectual development.* New York: Holt, Rinehart and Winston.

Rowan, B., Bossert, S. T., & Dwyer, D. C. (April, 1983). Research on effective schools: A cautionary note. *Educational Researcher,* 24–31.

Sizer, T. R. (1984). *Horace's compromise: The Dilemma of the American high school.* Boston: Houghton-Mifflin.

Weber, G. *Inner city children can be taught to read: Four successful schools.* (Occasional Paper No. 17) Washington, D.C.: Council for Basic Education, 1971.

CHAPTER 4

Observing Classroom Interaction

In Chapters 2 and 3 we placed you in the context of a specific school and classroom, and had you focus primarily on the physical and noninteractive dimensions of school and classroom phenomena: seating arrangements, a description of a schoolteacher's day, the location of various types of resource rooms, and so on. In this chapter, the observing becomes a bit more challenging as we focus your attention on various dynamic/interactive aspects of classroom life. There are many different types of interactions that occur daily between teachers and students, and from this wide range we have selected a set of interactions that meshes neatly with the major objectives of this chapter.

Our primary objective in this chapter is to put you in touch with the major elements of the contemporary teacher's day and role, namely lesson planning, lesson implementation (teaching), and classroom management. Planning, teaching, and evaluating lessons is the basic stuff of a teacher's career, and to aspire to become a teacher suggests that you want to be deeply involved with these basic teacher tasks. To help you make sure this is the case, our Core Activity will give you the opportunity to observe a wide range of lessons from several different types of teachers. This will include student teachers, teachers new to the profession, and teachers who have taught for four or more years. As noted below, this type of exposure should provide you with some valuable longitudinal and developmental insights into the career of teaching, as well as some basic perceptions about the student-teaching phase of teacher education, a phase you may already be curious about.

Beyond the Core Activity, which will be a time-consuming activity, we offer six carefully conceived activities that cover a wide range of interactive classroom situations. Each of these activities has a slightly different contribution to make to your overall awareness of the interactive nature of teaching and the complex nature of the classroom teacher's role. The suggested activities will place you in a position to code various forms of praise as they occur within several lessons, classify different types of questions, and observe transition periods, classroom management, learning climates, and the use of technology in the classroom. Each of the activities in this chapter has its own introduction and this introduction will help to clarify why this set of observation activities was selected to be included in this chapter. Let us turn now to the Core Activity with its introduction.

Activities for Chapter Four

THE CORE ACTIVITY (LESSON OBSERVATION)

As prospective teachers you should appreciate that if you enter the teaching profession, you will plan and teach thousands of lessons during the course of your career. In addition, a significant portion of the teacher-education program that prepares you for your career will be devoted to teaching you how to plan, implement, and evaluate lessons. In other words, planning and teaching lessons comprise at least two-thirds of the real work of teaching, and are therefore critical activities for prospective teachers to observe and contemplate. When professionals state that teaching is hard work, they typically have in mind the detailed thinking that precedes many lessons, and the large amounts of energy needed to enthusiastically deliver from six to 10 lessons a day.

Because of the fundamental importance of lesson planning and implementation, in this activity you will have the opportunity to observe as many as 15 lessons, five each from three different kinds of teachers. First, you will observe and discuss lesson planning with experienced teachers (teachers who have been teaching for four or more years), then you will observe new teachers (teachers in their first, second, or third year of teaching), and finally you will observe student teachers. Comparing and contrasting lessons taught, and points of view expressed, by these three types of teachers should help you to appreciate, first, that lesson-planning implementation is a critical part of a teacher's career at all phases, but also that it is done differently at different phases of a teacher's career. If you do not find this aspect of a teacher's role intriguing, it may be a sign that teaching is not the right career for you. We recognize that 15 observations may prove difficult for many of you, but note also that your observations can begin early in the quarter or semester and take place throughout your course of study.

The Observation Task(s)

On the pages immediately following, there is one set of classroom observation forms, one form to be used with an experienced teacher, one form to be used with new teachers, and the final form for use with student teachers. Your task is to observe an experienced teacher, new teacher, and a student teacher deliver a similar (not identical) type of lesson to a similar group of students in the same, or nearby, grade level, and to answer a number of the questions on the forms during the lesson and a few afterward. You should complete as many observations as possible, making duplicate copies of the experienced, new, and student-teacher forms as needed. You will note that a number of questions tie into the information shared in Chapter 3, our chapter on effective schools. If time permits, you should ask the observed teachers some questions about the lesson you have observed.

Core Activity

Lesson Observation Form One
(Experienced Teacher)

Your Name: _____ Participating Teacher: _____

Date: _____ Grade/Subject: _____ School: _____

During the Lesson

1. At the beginning of the lesson, did the teacher do anything to get the attention of the class? If yes, please describe.

   _____

   _____

   _____

2. At the beginning, or sometime during the lesson, did the teacher do something to get the students interested in the lesson they were about to experience or were experiencing? If yes, please describe.

   _____

   _____

   _____

3. What was the teacher's main instructional objective in this lesson (the skill or knowledge, etc., he or she was most interested in having the students learn in this lesson)?

   _____

   _____

   _____

   _____

   _____

4. What did the students learn in this lesson?

_____

_____

_____

_____

5. What were the students' reactions to the lesson (observe the class as a whole as well as two specific students)?

a) The whole class _____

_____

_____

_____

b) The two individuals _____

_____

_____

_____

6. Did the teacher in any way provide for individual differences? If yes, please describe.

_____

_____

_____

_____

7. In what specific ways did the teacher either praise the students or communicate high expectations to them?

_____

_____

_____

_____

8. What were some of the materials or visual aids the teacher used during the lesson? (Examples: chalkboard, posters, pictures, audio- or video-tapes, movies, computers, etc.)

_____

_____

_____

9. How exactly did the teacher close the lesson?

_____

_____

_____

10. What evidence did you see that suggested that the main instructional objective of this lesson had been achieved?

_____

_____

_____

_____

After the Lesson

1. What did you like about the way this lesson was taught?

_____

_____

_____

2. If you were going to teach this lesson to a similar group of students, what, if anything, would you change in the way this lesson was taught?

_____

_____

_____

_____

3. What questions do you have about the way the lesson was presented?

_____

_____

_____

_____

If you were able to speak to the teacher after the lesson, answer the following questions:

4. Did the teacher have a written lesson plan, or some type of written notes, to guide his or her instruction during the lesson? If yes, please describe the written notes. Are they in a lesson-plan book, or a separate sheet of paper in a lesson-plan format, on an index card, etc.?

_____

_____

_____

_____

5. Where did the content for this lesson come from?

☐ teacher's original research/lesson design

☐ a textbook

☐ one or more of the above

☐ a curriculum guide

Core Activity

Lesson Observation Form One
(New Teacher)

Your Name: _____   Participating Teacher: _____

Date: _____   Grade/Subject: _____   School: _____

During the Lesson

1. At the beginning of the lesson, did the teacher do anything to get the attention of the class? If yes, please describe.

   _____

   _____

   _____

2. At the beginning, or sometime during the lesson, did the teacher do something to get the students interested in the lesson they were about to experience or were experiencing? If yes, please describe.

   _____

   _____

   _____

3. What was the teacher's main instructional objective in this lesson (the skill or knowledge, etc., he or she was most interested in having the students learn in this lesson)?

   _____

   _____

   _____

   _____

   _____

4. What did the students learn in this lesson?

_____

_____

_____

_____

5. What were the students' reactions to the lesson (observe the class as a whole as well as two specific students)?

a) The whole class _____

_____

_____

_____

b) The two individuals _____

_____

_____

_____

6. Did the teacher in any way provide for individual differences? If yes, please describe.

_____

_____

_____

_____

7. In what specific ways did the teacher either praise the students or communicate high expectations to them?

_____

_____

_____

_____

8. What were some of the materials or visual aids the teacher used during the lesson? (Examples: chalkboard, posters, pictures, audio- or video-tapes, movies, computers, etc.)

_____

_____

_____

9. How exactly did the teacher close the lesson?

_____

_____

_____

10. What evidence did you see that suggested that the main instructional objective of this lesson was achieved?

_____

_____

_____

_____

After the Lesson

1. What did you like about the way this lesson was taught?

_____

_____

_____

2. If you were going to teach this lesson to a similar group of students, what, if anything, would you change in the way this lesson was taught?

_____

_____

_____

_____

3. What questions do you have about the way the lesson was presented?

_____

_____

_____

_____

If you were able to speak to the teacher after the lesson, answer the following questions:

4. Did the teacher have a written lesson plan, or some type of written notes, to guide his or her instruction during the lesson? If yes, please describe the written notes. Are they in a lesson-plan book, on a separate sheet of paper in a lesson-plan format, on an index card, etc.?

_____

_____

_____

_____

5. Where did the content for this lesson come from?

☐ teacher's original research/lesson design

☐ a curriculum guide

☐ a textbook

☐ one or more of the above

Core Activity

Lesson Observation Form One
(Student Teacher)

Your Name: _____ Participating Teacher: _____

Date: _____ Grade/Subject: _____ School: _____

During the Lesson

1. At the beginning of the lesson, did the student teacher do anything to get the attention of the class? If yes, please describe.

   _____

   _____

   _____

2. At the beginning, or sometime during the lesson, did the student teacher do something to get the students interested in the lesson they were about to experience or were experiencing? If yes, please describe.

   _____

   _____

   _____

3. What was the student teacher's main instructional objective in this lesson (the skill or knowledge, etc., he or she was most interested in having the students learn in this lesson)?

   _____

   _____

   _____

   _____

   _____

   _____

4. What did the students learn in this lesson?

_____

_____

_____

_____

5. What were the students' reactions to the lesson (observe the class as a whole as well as two specific students)?

a) The whole class _____

_____

_____

_____

b) The two individuals _____

_____

_____

_____

6. Did the student teacher in any way provide for individual differences? If yes, please describe.

_____

_____

_____

_____

7. In what specific ways did the student teacher either praise the students, or communicate high expectations to them?

_____

_____

_____

_____

8. What were some of the materials or visual aids the student teacher used during the lesson? (Examples: chalkboard, posters, pictures, audio- or videotapes, movies, computers, etc.)

_____

_____

_____

9. How exactly did the student teacher close the lesson?

_____

_____

_____

10. What evidence did you see that suggested that the main instructional objective of this lesson was achieved?

_____

_____

_____

_____

After the Lesson

1. What did you like about the way this lesson was taught?

_____

_____

_____

2. If you were going to teach this lesson to a similar group of students, what, if anything, would you change in the way this lesson was taught?

_____

_____

_____

_____

3. What questions do you have about the way the lesson was presented?

_____

_____

_____

_____

_____

If you were able to speak to the student teacher after the lesson, answer the following questions:

4. Did the student teacher have a written lesson plan, or some type of written notes, to guide his or her instruction during the lesson? If yes, please describe the written notes. Are they in a lesson-plan book, on a separate sheet of paper in a lesson-plan format, on an index card, etc.?

_____

_____

_____

_____

5. Where did the content for this lesson come from?

☐ teacher's original research/lesson design

☐ a curriculum guide

☐ a textbook

☐ one or more of the above

Comparison/Contrast Questions

1. What differences, if any, did you note between:
   a) the way the two teachers and one student teacher planned their lessons?

   _____

   _____

   b) the way the two teachers and one student teacher taught their lessons?

   _____

   _____

   _____

2. What, if anything, did the two teachers and one student teacher have in common as they taught the observed lessons?

   _____

   _____

3. From this set of observations, what did you discover/learn that was:

   a) interesting _____

   _____

   _____

   _____

   b) unanticipated _____

   _____

   _____

Suggested Activities for Chapter Four

Suggested Activity One
Teacher/Student Interaction

Increasingly, student teachers and in-service teachers are being asked to play a role in the professional development of another student teacher or in-service teacher. Sometimes this new "staff development" role involves observing a live or videotaped teaching episode. Activity One provides you with a simple, flexible observation instrument that will place you in a position to collect and communicate useful data about student/teacher interaction in various types of lessons.

Please note that we have provided two different interaction observation forms for use in classrooms with different seating arrangements. We have also included a third blank form because we expect that some of you will have to draw up your own seating chart to complete this activity. In addition, although in our task each symbol equals a specific teacher behavior, it should be well understood that at a later time you can modify the symbol system to allow you to focus on other teacher behaviors. For example, the dash (—) could stand for students who call out an answer without raising their hand, or it could stand for students who answer questions, and a plus (+) could stand for students who answer questions *and* receive praise. In a similar vein, this seating chart and symbol system could be used to compare the amount of teacher praise, and so on, received by boys as opposed to girls during a lesson.

The Task

Arrange to observe a teacher or student teacher who is teaching a large group (whole class) lesson in mathematics, social studies, English, and so on, and then follow the instructions listed below. Use the form that most closely approximates the seating arrangement in the classroom in which you are observing, or make up a new form on which to collect data if the seating arrangement in your room is divergent/unique.

Instructions for Using the Teacher/Student Interaction Observation Form

1. Observe the first 20 to 30 minutes of a particular lesson.
2. Familiarize yourself with the symbols listed below and where to place the symbols in the seating chart:
   (a) The dots will go in Box 1. Put a dot in the box when the teacher has given the student a chance to:
      (1) answer a question.

(2) give a report.

(3) receive help from teacher.

(b) The —'s will go in Box 2. Put a dash in Box 2 when the teacher requests or demands that a specific child stop doing something. (This is often referred to as a "desist" in the literature.)

(c) The +'s will go in Box 3. Put a plus mark in Box 3 where a student receives praise that is related to managing his or her behavior.

(d) The √'s will go in Box 4. Put a check in Box 4 where a student receives praise for instruction-related work.

3. Occasionally the teacher will give the entire class praise, or the opportunity to respond as an entire group. Use the boxes below the seating chart to record these whole-class behaviors.

(a) Put an X in the "total-class-responses" box when the teacher asks for a total-class response.

(b) Put an X in the "entire-class-receives-praise" box when this occurs.

4. On the seating chart, signify whether a boy or girl is seated there by putting a capital B or G above the box. At a later point, this will place you in a position to count up and analyze the data in terms of gender, if indeed you wish to do that. Other letters, of course, could be used to indicate ethnicity if you were interested in coding and quantifying that aspect of classroom interaction.

5. Fill out the comments portion of the *Interaction Observation Form.*

Teacher/Student Interaction Observation Form 1

Teacher's Name ————————————   Lesson Began ————————————

Observer's Name ————————————   Lesson Ended ————————————

Date ————————————————   Lesson Content ————————————
　　　　　　　　　　　　　　　　　　　(Math, Reading, etc.)

(Front of Room)

Row 1　　Row 2　　Row 3　　Row 4　　Row 5　　Row 6　　Row 7

BOX	
1	2
3	4

Opportunity for Total Class Response (X)　　Entire Class Receives Praise (X)

The Code

● = Student has opportunity to answer question, give a report, or receive help from the teacher (Box 1)

— = Teacher asks student to stop doing something (Box 2)

+ = Student receives praise related to managing his or her behavior (Box 3)

√ = Student receives praise that reinforces instruction (Box 4)

Teacher/Student Interaction Observation Form 2

Teacher's Name _____   Lesson Began _____

Observer's Name _____   Lesson Ended _____

Date _____   Lesson Content _____
                                              (Math, Reading, etc.)

(Front of Room)

Row 1	Row 2	Row 3	Row 4	Row 5	Row 6

BOX

1	2
3	4

Opportunity for Total Class Response (X)   Entire Class Receives Praise (X)

The Code

- ● = Student has opportunity to answer question, give a report, or receive help from the teacher (Box 1)
- — = Teacher asks student to stop doing something (Box 2)
- + = Student receives praise related to managing his or her behavior (Box 3)
- √ = Student receives praise that reinforces instruction (Box 4)

63

Teacher/Student Interaction Observation Form 3

Teacher's Name ————————————   Lesson Began ————————————

Observer's Name ————————————   Lesson Ended ————————————

Date ————————————————   Lesson Content ————————————
                                     (Math, Reading, etc.)

(Front of Room)

BOX

1	2
3	4

Opportunity for Total Class Response (X)   Entire Class Receives Praise (X)

The Code

- ● = Student has opportunity to answer question, give a report, or receive help from the teacher (Box 1)
- — = Teacher asks student to stop doing something (Box 2)
- + = Student receives praise related to managing his or her behavior (Box 3)
- √ = Student receives praise that reinforces instruction (Box 4)

Student Name _____ Date _____

1. Comments about the distribution of opportunity to respond, desist, and praise during this lesson:

   _____

   _____

   _____

   _____

   _____

   _____

2. Assuming that you were the principal of the school, or this student teacher's university supervisor, what questions might you raise with the teacher or student teacher if you had observed 10 lessons by this teacher and recorded interaction patterns similar to those you observed today?

   _____

   _____

   _____

   _____

   _____

   _____

Suggested Activity Two
Transition Periods

While it is quite appropriate to draw your attention to classroom lessons, and the management problems that sometimes occur during lessons, to more fully reveal to you the responsibilities of a classroom teacher, an observational activity related to transitional periods—the time before, after, and between lessons and other organized activities—is also appropriate. The questions and check-off items on the Transition Period Observation Form will clarify for you, first, that there is more to teaching than lesson planning, implementation, and evaluation, and second, that the organizational aspects of transition periods are just as important as the organizational aspects of lesson planning and implementation. Indeed, time saved during a routine or transition period is time that can be used to provide greater amounts of academic learning time for students.

Before using the transition-period form, some examples of transition-period times and activities should prove helpful. For example, during the elementary-school day in between lessons you might see a teacher walk her class out to the playground for a physical education activity or to the bathroom for a "watering" break; you might also see the class given a few minutes of free (decision-making) time, or some time to organize their homework packets to take home or to set up for the teacher's inspection. In a similar vein, you might see an elementary, junior-high-school or high-school teacher taking the roll, checking homework, lining the students up for dismissal or lunch, or simply telling students to turn to a specific page in a certain textbook and then look up when they are ready for the next lesson.

Use the Transition Period Observation Form on the same days as you carry out your Core Activity or Activity One to observe the way teachers manage time during transition periods. This form can be used for observations at any time of the day because lessons are always beginning and ending with transitions occurring before and after the lesson. You may find it interesting to know that research has demonstrated that teachers vary widely in their ability to efficiently organize their transition periods.

*Transition Period Observation Form**

Your Name: _____   Participating Teacher: _____

Date: _____   Grade/Subject: _____   School: _____

1. During the transition or routine period does the teacher do things that students could do for themselves?

   _____

   _____

   _____

2. Does the teacher give clear instructions about what to do next before moving into a transition period?

   _____

   _____

   _____

3. Is the transition period routine (taking attendance, lining up to sharpen pencils, moving to another seating arrangement, etc.) organized in an efficient manner, or can a more time-efficient procedure be developed?

   _____

   _____

   _____

4. Does the teacher circulate during transitions to handle individual needs? Does he or she take care of these before attempting to begin a new activity?

   _____

   _____

   _____

---

*Adaptation of two forms from LOOKING IN CLASSROOMS, Fourth Edition, by Thomas L. Good and Jere E. Brophy. Copyright © 1987 by Harper & Row, Publishers, Inc. Reprinted by permission of the publisher.

5. Does the teacher signal the end of a transition and the beginning of a structured activity properly, and quickly gain everyone's attention?

_____

_____

_____

6. Does the teacher use singing, background music, or any other creative device to add spice to the transition routine/period?

_____

_____

_____

_____

Check if applicable:

____ 1. Transitions occur too abruptly for students because the teacher fails to give advance warning or finish up reminders when needed.

____ 2. The teacher insists on unnecessary rituals or formalisms that cause delays or disruptions.

____ 3. The teacher is interrupted by individuals with the same problem or request; this could be handled by establishing a general rule or procedure (describe).

____ 4. Delays occur because frequently used materials are stored in hard-to-reach places.

____ 5. Poor traffic patterns result in pushing, bumping, or unnecessary noise.

____ 6. Delays occur while teacher prepares equipment or illustrates what should have been prepared earlier.

____ 7. Behavioral problems occur because of lack of structure during transition, or for other unidentified reasons.

Suggested Activity Three
Classroom Management

Classroom management and effective teaching are like breathing and exhaling; they are inextricably intertwined, part of an ongoing process, but often considered and discussed as separate processes. Indeed, for most teachers the words *classroom management* and *teaching* point to different areas of a classroom teacher's responsibilities. Further, in university teacher-education programs one will often find one specific course on classroom management and several courses on instruction of one kind or another. The classroom-management course is considered critical, and will usually contain readings, lectures, and discussions about how to: create and maintain good student behavior; arrange your classroom to promote effective instruction; get off to a good start at the beginning of the year; organize and manage the flow of information and paper that occurs before, during, and after instruction. Classroom management, in short, is about all the little and big things teachers do (tactics and strategies) to create a learning environment in which learning occurs smoothly and efficiently for a wide range of learners.

In recent years, educational research has validated a number of logical ideas about classroom management. For example, regarding good room arrangement, student teachers are taught to: keep high-traffic areas free of congestion; be sure all students are easily seen by the teacher; and make certain that all students can easily see instructional presentations. In a related vein, a consensus has grown around the use of rules in both elementary and secondary settings. Today, student teachers are taught how to develop a set of rules with their students, and are usually told to keep the number of rules to somewhere between five and eight rules.

While educational research has provided a set of validated tactics and strategies for classroom management, it is also true that teachers will always encounter behavioral situations that require special data collection, thinking, and solutions. Some exposure to these types of problems will make clear to you why the teaching profession needs bright people who can collect and synthesize data that is unique to a situation to come up with a variety of possible solutions as well as a plan of action.

The four different observation forms provided with Activity Three will allow you to observe classroom management from several vantage points. These forms can be used individually or together. For example, you might start out with Form A and note that a particular student is a significant behavior problem. In some elementary and in most secondary settings you could then choose to observe this same student in one or more different classrooms. Form B, which focuses on the effects that different teachers have on the same student, may prove helpful here, particularly if you are in a secondary-school setting. In the same vein, Form C, which helps you to collect case-study data on the pupil in one or more classrooms, provides yet another interesting type of data. Form D, which focuses on off-task and on-task behavior, is another good source of case-study data. Please note that the observation activities selected focus on the student-behavior aspect of classroom management. As indicated, classroom management is concerned with a wide-ranging set of classroom conditions and factors, all of which influence student behavior and learning. As you observe and interview in activities spelled out in various chapters in this text, you should maintain an active curiosity about classroom management.

You can begin this activity with Form A and observe in three or four class-rooms before choosing to use Form B, C, or D. Contrastingly, you might choose to start with Form A or B and use that form for all your observations.

Classroom Management Observation Form A

Your Name: _____   Participating Teacher: _____

Date: _____   Grade/Subject: _____   School: _____

Focus: Classroom Management in One Classroom

Data Collection

1. Did you notice any behavioral problems in this classroom? If yes, please describe.

   _____

   _____

   _____

2. How did the teacher respond to these problems?

   _____

   _____

   _____

3. What was the student's or students' immediate response to the teacher's interaction?

   _____

   _____

   _____

4. During the lesson, does the teacher make positive statements to the whole class or individual students to reward and encourage appropriate behavior? If yes, please include some of these positive statements below.

   _____

   _____

   _____

5. Did the teacher use what you would consider to be negative measures in response to student misbehavior? If so, please describe these measures below.

_____

_____

_____

_____

_____

Analysis

a) During this observation period, which management techniques appeared to be most effective?

_____

_____

_____

b) Which techniques, if any, appeared problematical or ineffective to you? What questions do you have about these techniques?

_____

_____

_____

_____

Classroom Management Observation Form B

Your Name: _____   Participating Teacher: _____

Date: _____   Grade/Subject: _____   School: _____

Focus: The Behavior of One Student in Several Different Classrooms

Data Collection

Observe one student's reactions in two or three different classes, noting his or her participation, facial expressions, body language, involvement in class, and relationships with peers and teachers.

1. How are these classrooms alike, and how are they different?

    _____

    _____

    _____

    _____

2. Is the mix of students roughly the same in all the classes, and if not, how are the groups different?

    _____

    _____

    _____

3. Does the student's behavior change from class to class? If yes, describe the change.

    _____

    _____

    _____

    _____

4. Does the change in behavior, either positive or negative, appear to be triggered by specific teacher behaviors? If yes, what teacher behaviors appear to be associated with the change in student behavior?

_____

_____

_____

_____

5. Is there any chance that your student's behavior change might be linked to the subject matter being taught? If yes, why do you think this *might* be the case?

_____

_____

_____

6. Are there any other possible explanations for the student's behavior? If yes, please spell out competing explanations that *might* be involved.

_____

_____

_____

7. What do different teachers do to encourage effective communication with the student you are observing, as well as other students?

_____

_____

_____

_____

8. What do you see teachers doing that appears to inhibit effective communication?

_____

_____

_____

_____

Analysis

If you were a school counselor providing suggestions to all the teachers this student interacted with, what suggestions *might* you provide?

_____

_____

_____

_____

_____

_____

Classroom Management Observation Form C*

Your Name: _____ Participating Teacher: _____

Date: _____ Grade/Subject: _____ School: _____

Focus: A Case Study of a Specific Student's Classroom Behavior**

Data Collection (Part One)

Use the codes on this page (A. Student Behavior, and B. Apparent Cause) to record the student's behavior at five-minute intervals and link it to antecedent causes when possible. Observe the student with more than one teacher, and in more than one instructional setting before filling out Part Two of form C.

	CODES	
TIME	A	B
1. ___	___ ___
2. ___	___ ___
3. ___	___ ___
4. ___	___ ___
5. ___	___ ___
6. ___	___ ___
7. ___	___ ___
8. ___	___ ___
9. ___	___ ___
10. ___	___ ___
11. ___	___ ___
12. ___	___ ___
13. ___	___ ___
14. ___	___ ___
15. ___	___ ___
16. ___	___ ___
17. ___	___ ___
18. ___	___ ___
19. ___	___ ___
20. ___	___ ___
21. ___	___ ___
22. ___	___ ___
23. ___	___ ___
24. ___	___ ___
25. ___	___ ___
26. ___	___ ___
27. ___	___ ___
28. ___	___ ___
29. ___	___ ___
30. ___	___ ___
31. ___	___ ___

A. Student Behavior

a. Pays attention or actively works at assignment
b. Stares in space or closes eyes
c. Fidgets, taps, amuses self
d. Distracts others—entertains, jokes
e. Distracts others—questions, seeks help,
f. Investigates
g. Distracts others—attacks or teases
h. Leaves seat—goes to teacher
i. Leaves seat—wanders, runs, plays
j. Leaves seat—does approved action (what?)
k. Leaves seat—does forbidden action (what?)
l. Calls out answer
m. Calls out irrelevant comment (what?)
n. Calls out comment about teacher (what?)
o. Deliberately causes disruption
p. Destroys property (whose? what?)
q. Leaves room without permission
r. Other (specify)

B. Apparent Cause
What triggered the behavior?
a. No observable cause—suddenly began acting out
b. Appeared stumped/frustrated and gave up
c. Finished work, had nothing to do
d. Distracted/bothered by classmate (who?)
e. Asked to respond or perform by teacher
f. Teacher checks or asks about progress on assigned work
g. Teacher calls for attention or return to work
h. Teacher praise (for what?)
i. Teacher criticism (for what?)
j. Teacher praises or rewards another student
k. Teacher criticizes or punishes another student

---

*Adaptation of two forms from LOOKING IN CLASSROOMS, Fourth Edition, by Thomas L. Good and Jere E. Brophy. Copyright © 1987 by Harper & Row, Publishers, Inc. Reprinted by permission of the publisher.
**Please note that this activity will have to be cleared by the school principal, who will direct you toward specific classrooms.

32. ____   ____ ____   l. Teacher refuses or delays permission request
33. ____   ____ ____   m. Student appears to be bored
34. ____   ____ ____   n. Student appears to be searching
35. ____   ____ ____   o. Other (specify)
36. ____   ____ ____
37. ____   ____ ____
38. ____   ____ ____
39. ____   ____ ____   Notes: _____
40. ____   ____ ____   _____

Data Collection (Part Two)

Record any information relevant to the following points.

Student's Emotional Response

1. Complains (He or she is disliked, picked on, left out, not getting share, unjustly blamed, ridiculed, asked to do what he or she can't do or has already done):

   _____

   _____

   _____

2. Posturing behavior (threats, obscenities, challenging or denying teacher's authority):

   _____

   _____

   _____

3. Defense mechanisms (silence, pouting, mocking politeness or agreement, appears ashamed or angry, talks back or laughs, says "I don't care," rationalizes, blames others, tries to cajole or change subject):

   _____

   _____

   _____

Check if Applicable

_____ 1. Teacher tends to overreact to student's misbehavior

_____ 2. Student's misbehavior usually leads to affection or reward from the teacher

_____ 3. Student usually acts out for no apparent reason

_____ 4. Student usually acts out when idle or unable to do assignments

_____ 5. Student usually acts out when distracted by another child

_____ 6. Student usually acts out in response to the teacher's behavior

Positive Behavior

1. Note the student's changes in behavior over time. When is he or she most attentive? What topics or situations seem to interest the student?

   _____

   _____

2. What questions does the student raise his or her hand to answer?

   _____

   _____

3. What work assignments does the student diligently try to do well?

   _____

   _____

4. What activities does the student select if given a choice?

   _____

   _____

Analysis

From the data you have collected about this student, do you see any patterns that might lead to recommendations for the student's teachers if you were a counselor as opposed to a prospective teacher? If so, please describe the patterns.

_____

_____

_____

_____

Classroom Management Observation Form D

Your Name: _____ Participating Teacher: _____

Date: _____ Grade/Subject: _____ School: _____

First Name of Observed Student: _____

Focus: Measuring Individual Students' Academic Engaged Time by Recording Students' On-Task and Off-Task Behavior

Data Collection

Identify the student(s) you intend to observe before the observation day. Observe the first student on your list; if that student is absent, observe the second student on your list. Observe each student for a period of 30 minutes during a lesson. At the end of each minute during the lesson, observe the student and mark the activity below that best describes the student's behavior. When finished, you will have recorded 30 observations. Put a check in the appropriate row to identify the observed activity. When the 30-minute observation period is completed, add up the checks in each row, total the on- and off-task behavior, and then work out the percentage for off- and on-task behavior.

On-Task Behavior

The student is engaged in tasks related to academic material. This may include: listening to the teacher, asking questions, completing an assignment, and so on.

Record Checks Here

▢ = Total Number of Checks for On-Task Behavior   ▢ = % On-Task Academic Behavior*

Off-Task Behavior

Record Checks Here

1. Daydreaming _____
2. Socializing _____
3. Doodling _____
4. Playing with other students _____
5. General misbehavior _____
6. Waiting for assistance _____
7. Sharpening pencil _____

---

*For example, if there were 10 checks for on-task behavior, and 20 checks for off-task behavior, the respective percentages would be 33% and 67%. Roughly speaking, one could say that this student had a 33% academic-engaged rate during this lesson.

8. Getting materials needed for lesson

9. Getting a drink of water

10. Off to the bathroom

11. Interrupted or distracted from lesson by an intercom message, fire drill, another student, and so on

☐ = Total Number of Checks for Off-Task Behavior

☐ = % On-Task Academic Behavior

Suggested Activity Four
Classroom Arrangement

The working, teaching, and learning environments that teachers create for students vary greatly across grades and within grades. To gain insight into the physical as well as instructional dimensions and implications of this range, complete one or more of the following tasks.

1. Gain permission to visit a large number of classrooms in a single school. Spend approximately 10 to 15 minutes in each class taking general notes about bulletin boards, file cabinets, chalkboard space, seating arrangement, aesthetic appeal, and so on. Spend the bulk of your time in the classroom just looking and trying to get a feel for the atmosphere and/or the learning climate.

2. After you have visited a large number of classes, compare and contrast three or more of the classrooms that you found to be interesting in terms of classroom design.

3. Arrange to observe a lesson in a room that you felt was well organized and tastefully arranged, and a lesson in a classroom that was poorly organized and less tastefully arranged. Use the lesson observation form from the core activity to collect data on the lessons. After data collection, compare and contrast the two lessons. Was there any relationship between the quality of classroom design and the quality of lesson design and implementation?

Suggested Activity Five
Questioning

To help you gain a well-rounded view of the career you are considering, we have encouraged you to observe as much teaching as possible because the act of planning and implementing lessons is a fundamental and pervasive dimension of teaching. In the same vein, we will now provide you with the opportunity to take a closer look at a significant component of lesson planning and lesson execution, namely the component that concerns question creation and questioning itself.

The development of *patterns* of questions that have appropriate variety, as well as single questions that are intriguing, challenging, and original is a satisfying aspect of teaching. However, research has consistently demonstrated that many teachers deliver patterns or sets of questions that are predominantly lower order, that is, questions that deal with memorization and factual recall of information. These memory-level questions do not require students to do something challenging with the retrieved information (e.g., interpret, analyze, compare and contrast, synthesize, evaluate, create). Interestingly, some educational writers have argued that effective teaching for certain groups of students will involve high percentages of factual, lower-order questions. At the same time, the wisdom of teaching (accumulated practical experience) indicates that most students benefit from judicious mixtures of higher-order and lower-order questions, as well as the opportunity to develop and ask their own interesting questions. The forms utilized in this activity will introduce you to a tool for determining the percentage of lower-order and higher-order questions asked by teacher and students in a selected lesson, as well as the teacher's questioning rate (the number of questions asked per minute). If you proceed into the final phases of a teacher-preparation program, you will be able to utilize this instrument to work out the ratio of higher- to lower-order questions in your own (tape-recorded) lessons. The second observation in this activity will place you in a position to observe the effects of "teacher wait time" on the level of oral participation in selected classrooms and lessons. The research base on wait time dates back to the pioneering work of Mary Budd Rowe (1974) in the early 1970s. Rowe suggested that slowing down the pace of question-and-answer classroom communication would have a variety of positive results. Recently conducted research supports this contention (Tobin, 1986; 1987). When students are given more time to think after a question is asked, more students are able to respond, the length of their remarks increases, and the students are more likely to listen and respond to each other. A good deal of research has shown that many teachers, after asking a question, wait less than a second before rephrasing the question, answering it themselves, or asking another question. Staff development efforts in this area have attempted to train teachers to expand their wait time to three or more seconds between the question and the next teacher move. It will be interesting to see what results from your own observations in this area.

The Higher-Order/Lower-Order Questioning Analysis Form

Your Name: _____   Participating Teacher: _____

Date: _____   Grade/Subject: _____   School: _____

Focus: The ratio of Lower-Order and Higher-Order Questions Asked in Specific Lessons and the Teacher's Questioning Rate

Information

Lower-order questions deal with memorization and recall of factual information. The student does not use the information in any way (to apply, analyze, evaluate, etc.). The student is asked to retrieve from his memory bank certain information.

Examples of lower-order questions:

1. Who was the first president of the United States of America?
2. Which American president went into politics after a career in acting?
3. In which American city is the White House located?
4. Yesterday we discussed the factors that led to the Civil War. Who remembers which factor was considered to be most important?

Higher-order questions require students to use the information recalled in some manner—such as explaining its meaning, comparing or contrasting it to something else, making a generalization, applying it to solve a problem, analyzing the information, synthesizing or evaluating the information.

Examples of higher-order questions and tasks:

1. What does this poem mean to you?
2. Do you think the poet embedded a special message in the poem? If so, what is it?
3. Why do you think Ronald Reagan was such a popular, well-liked, president?
4. Which generalization about the factors contributing to the Civil War appears most accurate to you? Explain your choice.
5. If you pull all of this information together, which solutions to the problem emerge?

Data Collection

Nature and Number of Teacher Questions

1. Select a typical 30-minute segment of teacher–student interaction and tape-record the teaching episode. Then record on two separate sheets of paper the questions asked by the teacher and the questions asked by the students.
2. How many teacher questions were higher-order thought questions?

3. How many teacher questions were lower-order memory questions?

4. What was the percentage of higher-order questions asked by the teacher?

$$\frac{\text{higher-order questions}}{\text{total questions}} = \text{percentage}$$

5. What was the rate of question asking by the teacher?

$$\frac{\text{total questions asked}}{30 \text{ minutes}} = \text{teacher questions per minute}$$

6. How many of these student questions were higher-order thought questions?

7. How many of these questions were lower-order memory questions?

8. What was the percentage of higher-order questions asked by the students?

$$\frac{\text{higher-order questions}}{\text{total questions}} = \text{percentage}$$

9. What was the rate of question asking by all students? What was the average rate of question asking by a single student?

$$\text{total student rate} = \frac{\text{total questions asked}}{30 \text{ minutes}}$$
$$= \text{total student questions per minute}$$

$$\text{average student rate} = \frac{\text{total student questions per minute}}{\text{number of students in the class}}$$

Analysis

1. Compare the questioning rates and questioning ratios (higher-order to lower-order) of teacher and students in this lesson. What observations derive from this comparison?

2. Examine the content, clarity, and sequence of the teacher's questions. What observations derive from this analysis? Does this analysis lead to observations that are similar to or different from the observations derived from analysis of questioning rate and ratio?

3. If you were this teacher's coach or supervisor, would you have any advice to give about the questions in this lesson? If so, please spell out.

The Teacher's Questions

1. _____
2. _____
3. _____
4. _____
5. _____
6. _____
7. _____
8. _____
9. _____
10. _____
11. _____
12. _____
13. _____
14. _____
15. _____
16. _____
17. _____
18. _____
19. _____
20. _____
21. _____
22. _____
23. _____
24. _____
25. _____

The Student's Questions

1. _____
2. _____
3. _____
4. _____
5. _____
6. _____
7. _____
8. _____
9. _____
10. _____
11. _____
12. _____
13. _____
14. _____
15. _____
16. _____
17. _____
18. _____
19. _____
20. _____

The Wait Time in Questioning Analysis Form

Your Name: _____   Participating Teacher: _____

Date: _____   Grade/Subject: _____   School: _____

Focus: Analysis of Wait Time in Questioning

Information

Research has demonstrated that the number of seconds a teacher waits after asking a question dramatically influences the range of student response in a classroom (the number of pupils who want to orally respond) *and* the length of individual oral responses. The wait time after the student's response is another influential variable, but in this activity, we will focus on the teacher's wait time after he or she has asked a question. Parenthetically, three seconds is *generally* considered to be a productive amount of wait time.

Data Collection

Use a stop watch and the audiotape of the teaching episode from the previous activity to answer the following questions:

1. What is the teacher's *average* wait time for lower-order questions?
2. What is the teacher's *average* wait time for higher-order questions?
3. What is the teacher's overall wait time for all questions?
4. Was the teacher's wait time for lower-order and higher-order questions generally consistent, or did he or she have a combination of very short (less than a second) and very long (five to 15 seconds) wait times?
5. Did the student's responses appear to be affected by the teacher's wait time?

Analysis

1. What observations derive from your comparison of wait time for lower-order versus higher-order questions?
2. If you were this teacher's coach or supervisor, would you have any wait time advice to offer this teacher? If so, spell out the advice.
3. What other factors, beyond teacher time, do you think might cause a wide range of students to want to give an oral response?

Suggested Activity Six

Uses of Technology in Instruction

In the Core Activity we said that planning and teaching lessons comprised at least two-thirds of the real work of teaching. With this statement we wanted to remind prospective teachers that a lot of important teaching takes place in between and after formal lessons as teachers engage in developing a variety of significant noninstructional activities and personal relationships with students. Their teaching will increasingly take place in learning environments filled with interactive technical devices (televisions, tape recorders, computers, laser disks, etc.). The point here is that in the future, teachers will increasingly deliver instruction via well-designed total learning environments in addition to well-conceived individual lessons. For this reason in Activity Six we will encourage the observation of teachers who carry on instruction in carefully designed technological learning environments. Although many elementary schools still have most students visit one learning or computer lab for a specified number of minutes a day, during your career as a teacher, your classroom will increasingly take on characteristics of the computer lab you will visit.

The Observation Task

On your own, or with the help of your professor, identify a classroom, learning laboratory, or computer lab, and arrange to observe instruction in this learning environment for several hours. Where possible:

1. Arrange to conduct your observation in a setting in which the instructor has a reputation for creative use of interactive technology (computers, videotape machines, television, etc.).
2. Observe different-age children learning in these technological learning environments.
3. Receive permission to talk with (interview) children about their learning *during* the class period.

Technology in the Classroom Observation Form

Your Name: _____   Participating Teacher: _____

Date: _____   Grade/Subject: _____   School: _____

Focus: The Use of Technlogy to Deliver Various Forms of Individualized Instruction

Data Collection

1. What did the teacher do in this learning laboratory or classroom?

   (a) _____

   _____

   (b) _____

   _____

   (c) _____

   _____

   (d) _____

   _____

2. In what ways did the teacher interact with students in this learning environment?

   _____

   _____

   _____

   _____

3. What things were students doing in this classroom as they interacted with technology?

   _____

   _____

   _____

   _____

4. What kinds of individual or group learning activities were students engaged in while you were observing them?

_____

_____

_____

5. Did the class or learning laboratory you were observing appear to have classroom-management or discipline problems? If yes, please describe them.

_____

_____

_____

6. To what extent were the students in this classroom or learning lab engrossed in the activity (on-task) as opposed to being off-task (in one way or another)?

_____

_____

_____

7. What were students learning in this classroom or learning environment?

_____

_____

_____

8. Were the students in this learning laboratory or class engaged in higher-level tasks (analyzing, interpreting, evaluating, creating, problem creating, problem solving)?

_____

_____

_____

Comparison, Contrast, and Analysis

1. What were the significant differences between this classroom or learning environment and other classrooms you have recently observed?

_____

_____

_____

_____

_____

2. Were you excited by what you observed in this classroom or learning environment? If yes, why? If not, why not?

_____

_____

_____

_____

_____

3. Does the teacher's role appear to change in this kind of learning environment? If yes, how are the role(s) of the teacher different in this class from other classrooms you have recently observed?

_____

_____

_____

_____

_____

4. If children's learning behavior in this classroom or learning environment was different from students you observed in other types of classrooms, to what do you attribute this difference?

_____

_____

_____

_____

5. To what extent did the students in this class appear to be *controlled* by the technology, as opposed to being in a position to use the technology to have control over their learning process?

_____

_____

_____

_____

_____

Student Name _____   Date _____

Journal Entry

Inasmuch as this chapter attempted to put you in close contact with a set of significant day-to-day responsibilities of classroom teachers, your journal entry should concentrate on what you have learned about these important areas of classroom teaching. More specifically, your entry should focus on what you have learned about:

1. Lesson planning and lesson implementation in general;
2. Lesson planning and implementation at different stages in a teacher's career;
3. Classroom management;
4. Classroom questioning;
5. Student/teacher interaction and dialogue; and
6. Technology in the learning environment.

_____
_____
_____
_____
_____
_____
_____
_____
_____
_____
_____
_____
_____
_____

Questions for Discussion

1. You have had the opportunity to observe many different lessons in this chapter. As you consider these lessons as a group, what characteristic of the lessons was memorable, intriguing, or surprising to you, and why was this the case?

2. In this chapter, you have had the opportunity to observe teachers with varying levels of experience. What struck you as noteworthy about the comparative as well as individual performance of these teachers?

3. Did you find the observation of lessons taught by teachers with varying levels of experience to be a worthwhile task? If yes, what did you learn that was helpful?

4. Most educational researchers describe the American classroom as a complex place.

    (a) Did your observations of classroom interaction leave you with this impression?

    (b) If yes, as a prospective teacher, how did this complexity make you feel?

    (c) If not, what feelings are associated with your observations of classroom interaction?

5. The interaction that occurs between one teacher and 25 to 35 students in the context of a lesson is a special type of patterned interaction and communication, but this pattern is not unlike the patterned interaction that occurs in several other organizational settings. What did the classroom interaction you observed remind you of, if anything? In what ways was it, the classroom interaction, similar to the interaction you have observed or experienced in another setting? Does this similarity have any implications for your future career as a teacher? If yes, please identify and discuss.

References

Rowe, M. B. (1974). Wait-time and rewards as instructional variables, their influences on language, logic, and fate control. *Journal of Research in Science Teaching,* 11(2), 81–94.

Tobin, K. (Summer, 1986). Effects of teacher wait-time on discourse characteristics in math and language arts classrooms. *American Educational Research Journal,* 23(2), 191–200.

Tobin, K. (1987). The role of wait time in higher cognitive level learning. *Review of Educational Research,* 57(1), 69–95.

C H A P T E R 5

Developing Interviewing Skills

This chapter is one of several in this text in which you will utilize interview-ing. You will focus on classroom teachers as a source of information, but will also have the opportunity to practice interviewing with classmates, student teachers, and university professors. Before placing you in the interview set-ting, we will provide you with specific information on *how* and *whom* to inter-view in K–12 settings.

It is worth noting that all of the interview tasks in this text are appropriate because they have you, a prospective teacher, utilizing a dynamic, exciting, teaching-learning strategy (interviewing) to conduct teaching-related research right at the beginning of your career. These interview activities will require you to be outgoing, articulate, well-organized, patient, and a good listener. The time you put into the preparation and implementation of these inter-views will be time that is well invested. You will see that the interviews you carry out will expand and modify the interpretations you placed on various observed events. Many of you will be assigned to a teacher, or spend more time with one teacher, during your early field experience, and through the interview process you may well engage in your first face-to-face professional exchange with a K–12 practitioner. With these interviews, you will begin your initiation into the rich dialogue about teaching that is beginning to occur in many K–12 programs in this era of educational reform.

We will focus on the structured interview and its most useful derivative, the semistructured interview, in this chapter. We choose this focus even though it is predictable that during the course of your teacher-education pro-gram you will derive much useful information from the informal, unplanned, spontaneous discussions you will have with teachers in a variety of school and nonschool settings. While informal interviews definitely have their time and place, the semistructured interview is a particularly appropriate tool for pro-spective teachers who are trying to make contact with professional educators in the ultra-busy world that teachers inhabit. This will be even more true for the outstanding teachers we encourage you to seek out; in most cases they will have gotten their reputations because of the extra time and energy they put into their classrooms. This type of teacher will find it difficult to make time for a meandering, unfocused interview. You will also discover that the semistructured, preplanned interview will work for you, first in helping to get you the interview, and then in helping you derive the maximum amount of useful information in what will usually be a short period of time, say 30 to 40 minutes. Let us now take a closer look at structured and semistructured interviews.

The Structured Interview

The structured interview has several distinctive characteristics. For example, in a structured interview the questions will be written out in advance, and the phrasing and content of the questions will be checked to make sure the questions are clear and easy to interpret. In addition, you will arrange the questions in what appears to be a sequential, logical manner; will try to match the number of questions in the interview schedule to the amount of time planned for the interview; and will write out a statement explaining the purpose of the interview. Once the questions have been selected, tried out on friends, and put into their final form, the questions will be laid out on a note pad, with a page left for each question, to facilitate note taking during the interview.

When the questions have been identified, and you know approximately how much time you will need for the interview, and have carefully written out the purpose of the interview, you are ready to make phone contact with the teacher for the purpose of arranging a time and place for the interview. The first contact will likely be with a school secretary, and you should sound organized, polite, *and* appreciative as the secretary tries to find out when the teacher will have a break during the day. Once contact has been made with the teacher, you should provide the teacher with (or indicate):

1. Your name and position within a specific teacher-education program (are you a sophomore at Bowling Green University, or a postbaccalaureate candidate about to enter the teacher-education program, etc.);
2. That you would like to arrange a brief 20- or 30-minute interview;
3. The kinds of questions you intend to ask (two or three examples of your questions) and the purpose of the interview; and
4. The kind of flexibility you have for the interview ("I can show up at your school between noon and 2:00 p.m. on Mondays, Wednesdays, and Fridays").

Before discussing the actual questions that make up a structured interview, it should be understood that during the course of the interview it is natural and appropriate for the structured interview to be transformed into a semi-structured one. This transformation occurs when you, the interviewer, choose to build on the answer to one question by asking a new, unplanned question. This is analogous to the situation that occurs every day in thousands of classrooms across the world when teachers diverge from their lesson plans to seize upon that uniquely fertile circumstance that educators commonly call the "teachable" moment. In the context of interviews carried out by novice interviewers, an apt label for the transition to the semistructured interview would be the "questionable" moment. Such divergence is extremely practical and highly recommended. The amount of time spent on the interview will likely be the same. Some preplanned questions may not get asked, but they can be included in your next interview. You will find that your interview will be more enjoyable and probably more revealing when you seize the opportunity to add questions to your preplanned structured interview.

> *In what ways are interviewing skills essential to effective communication between teachers and parents, students, and other teachers?*

"Well, you see, Mrs. Smith, the reason your son is doing poorly in school is that he's dumb."

used with permission of the cartoonist—Tom McCally

The Interview Questions

The reader might well ask what comes first, the teacher or the interview? As noted earlier, we recommend that you develop your interview first, and then use your questions and interview rationale to help you land interviews with educators who are already busy. However, it would be practical to be thinking about the kind of teacher you want to interview as you develop your questions. For example, you might decide that your first interview will be with a kindergarten teacher as opposed to a sixth-grade teacher, or a junior-high-school English teacher as opposed to a high-school English, speech, or history teacher. Focusing in on a particular category of teacher will make it easier to generate grade-level-specific and course-content-specific questions; these are questions that would only make sense to a specific grade-level teacher, or teacher of a specific course. Examples of tenth-grade biology questions are:

1. What kinds of laboratory experiences are a common part of the curriculum at this high school?

2. To what extent is the high-school biology curriculum career oriented?

After focusing in on a particular type of teacher, the next logical step in the interview development process is to brainstorm and generate a randomly ordered set of questions. Once the questions exist, the sequencing and refining process can begin. At this point the reader may be wondering: Do I generate these questions all by myself? Typically, the answer is "no." There are at least five different sources of questions, and the five, in combination, will produce an abundant yield of appropriate questions. These sources include: the classrooms you observe in; the professors in your teacher-education program; your own curiosity; sample questions included in this text (see, for example, Table 5.1); and finally, sharing questions with your fellow students, possibly in brainstorming sessions.

To illustrate more clearly how a structured interview is developed, we are going to walk you through the development process in a step-by-step fashion. As you proceed, you will draw on a set of general questions for structured interviews (see Table 5.1). This set of questions will include personal background questions that we suggest you use at the beginning of all, or most, teacher interviews.

The Structured Interview Development Process

I.   First, pick a certain category of teacher. For this example our category will be *sixth-grade teacher*.

II. Next, generate a list of questions.

A. Select questions from Table 5.1. For our example, we will select the following questions from Table 5.1 (1, 2, 4, 7, 9, 10, 11, 12, 14, 15).

B. Add other questions that stem from your observations in upper-grade elementary-school classrooms, your own curiosity, and suggestions from your professors and fellow students. Questions such as the ones below will probably result:

1. Why is it that in several classes I have observed, reading is taught in small groups and math in large groups? (Based on observation in other classrooms.)

2. Why do you have the children seated in little clusters of fours with their desks facing each other? (Based on observation in the interviewee's classroom.)

3. Is the sixth grade a unique or special grade to teach? And if so, what makes it special? In what ways is it different than the fifth grade?

4. Do you have textbooks to help you teach all the separate elementary-school content areas?

5. Does the school perceive some content areas to be more important than others? How does this attitude influence the actual delivery of the school curriculum?

6. How does teaching in the upper-elementary grades differ from teaching in the lower grades?

7. When did you first discover that you were going to be an upper-elementary teacher?

III. Step three is the sequencing and refining step. We will arbitrarily select a 15-question limit for this structured interview. This means we could select five of the questions directly above, integrate them with the 10 questions from Table 5.1, and then work out a logical sequence. Here are 15 questions listed in random order. Rearrange them to create your own logical sequence, and then compare it with the sequential structured-interview schedule we have created. Discuss any differences with fellow students and/or your instructor.

The Random List

a. Why is it that reading is taught in small groups in your class, and math in large groups? (Based on prior observation in the teacher's class.)

b. What helped you decide to become a teacher, and what helped you choose to remain a teacher?

c. How do you think the role of teacher may change in the next five years?

d. Do you consider teaching to be a challenging profession, in the positive sense of the word? And, if so, what challenges have made teaching an interesting career for you?

e. How does teaching in the sixth grade differ from teaching in the first grade?

f. What have you found most satisfying in your career in teaching?

g. What is the job like after school is out? Do you find yourself bringing home school work after school, or on weekends?

h. Do school administrators think that some content areas are more important than others? How do these beliefs influence the actual content and delivery of the school curriculum?

i. Before asking you more specific questions about the teaching profession, could you tell me a bit about your background in teaching?

(1) Years of experience?

(2) Grade levels taught?

(3) Numbers of years in this school? School district?

TABLE 5.1
General Questions for Structured Interviews

1. Before asking you more specific questions about the teaching profession, could you tell me a bit about your background as a teacher? (a) Years of experience? (b) Grade levels taught? (c) Numbers of years teaching at this school . . . in this school district?
2. What have you found most satisfying in your career in teaching?
3. What has been the most unsatisfying element in your teaching career?
4. In the positive sense of the word, do you consider teaching to be a challenging profession? And, if so, what challenges have made teaching an interesting career for you?
5. Do you consider teaching to be a profession? Why? Why not?
6. What do you do to keep yourself rejuvenated or enthusiastic about teaching?
7. (a) Do you belong to a teachers' organization, and if yes, which one(s)?
   (b) How do these organizations help teachers?
   (c) Is there a negative side to teachers' organizations?
8. If you were starting out all over, and just about to begin a teacher-education program, on which teaching skills or areas of knowledge would you place extra effort?
9. What important changes have occurred in the profession of teaching during your teaching career?
10. How do you think the role of teacher may change in the next five to 10 years?
11. During your career in teaching, has teaching become a more interesting job? A more difficult job? What has made it more interesting and/or more difficult?
12. What is the job like after school is out? Do you find yourself bringing home school work after school, or on weekends? On the average, how many hours per week do you put into your teaching?
13. Are computers widely used in your school? In your classroom? If so, for what purpose?
14. Are there specific books, courses, or workshop experiences that have been particularly meaningful to you as a teacher? If so, could you briefly describe them?
15. What helped you decide to become a teacher, and what helped you choose to remain a teacher?
16. How did you wind up teaching at your current grade level? If you had the opportunity to start all over again, would you obtain a credential to teach at another level, say, high school instead of elementary school?
17. What do you do that is particularly effective with students?
18. Would you recommend teaching as a career for your own children? Why? Why not?
19. What advice would you give to someone like me, someone who is at an early stage of the teacher-training process?

j. (1) Do you belong to a teachers' organization, and if so, which one(s)?

(2) How do these organizations help teachers?

(3) Do they create any problems for the profession?

k. When did you first discover that you were going to be an upper-elementary teacher?

l. What important changes in the teaching profession have occurred during your teaching career?

m. Do you have textbooks to help you teach all the separate elementary-school content areas?

n. During your career in teaching, has teaching become a more interesting job? A more difficult job? What has made it more interesting or more difficult?

o. What advice would you give to a student considering a career in teaching in today's world?

The Sequenced Structured Interview Schedule

1. Before asking you more specific questions about the teaching profession, could you tell me a bit about your background in teaching? (a) Years of experience? (b) Grade levels taught? (c) Number of years teaching at this school . . . in this school district?

2. What have you found most satisfying in your career in teaching?

3. Do you consider teaching to be a challenging profession, in the positive sense of the word? And, if so, what challenges have made teaching an interesting career for you?

4. What important changes in the teaching profession have occurred during your teaching career?

5. How do you think the role of teacher may change in the next five to 10 years?

6. During your career in teaching, has teaching become a more interesting job? A more difficult job? What has made it more interesting and/or more difficult?

7. What is the job like after school is out? Do you find yourself bringing home school work after school, or on weekends?

8. (a) Do you belong to a teachers' organization, and if yes, which one(s)?

(b) How do these organizations help teachers?

(c) Do they create any problems for the profession?

9. What helped you decide to become a teacher, and what helped you choose to remain a teacher?

10. How does teaching in the sixth grade differ from teaching in the first grade?

11. When did you first discover that you were going to be an upper-elementary teacher?

12. Do you have textbooks to help you teach all the separate elementary-school content areas?

13. Do school administrators think that some content areas are more important than others? How do these beliefs influence the actual content and delivery of the school curriculum?

14. Why is it that reading is taught in small groups in your class, and math in large groups? (Based on prior observation in the teacher's class.)

15. What advice would you give to a student considering a career in teaching in today's world?

Now that you have your sequenced questions, you are ready to write down the purpose of your interview, or what we shall call your interview rationale. When you make your first contact with the teacher, you will use this short statement to help you win your interview with a busy educator. Following is an example of an interview rationale for the listed sequence of questions. Please note that your statement should be direct and to the point.

Interview Rationale Example

"My purpose in seeking this interview is to learn more about the teaching profession from people in the profession. I want to learn as much as I can about teaching as a possible career for myself."

Interview Guidelines

As in most complex endeavors, there are a few rules or guidelines in interviewing that, if followed, will help you have a positive experience. Following, we will list some "do's" and "don'ts" for interviewing. The "do's" will come first:

1. Be aware as you go out for your interviews that you represent your teacher-education program, as well as yourself.

2. Realize that both you and your teacher-education program are, or should be, striving to develop and maintain a positive reputation with the teachers in your region, and therefore represent yourself and your program well.

3. Treat the data you collect as semiconfidential information. You will share observations related to your data with your professors and fellow students, but you need not and should not use the teacher's name in these discussions. There is no instructional advantage in using such names, but there is the clear possibility that some misunderstanding may develop if teachers come to believe that they are being unprofessionally, and unethically, evaluated.

4. Be exceedingly polite and patient as you interact with your interviewee and other school personnel.

5. Dress professionally for your interview, and in your particular region find out what that means.

6. Be better than punctual, and come well organized and prepared to take notes.

7. On the day before the interview, call the school to leave a polite reminder about the interview. You can ask a school secretary to place a brief written note in the teacher's mailbox:

   "Dear Mr./Ms. Smith, I am looking forward to our interview tomorrow and will meet you at your room as planned."

8. Conduct your interview in a private setting: the teacher's classroom, the school library, and so on.

9. Follow up the interview with a brief thank-you note. You can write it in advance and drop it off in the teacher's mailbox as you leave the school.

A list of "don'ts" follows:

1. Don't bring a tape recorder to use or even ask to use a tape recorder on your first visit; our experience suggests that the pressure of the tape recorder, during the first meeting, serves to make the interview excessively formal.

2. Don't repeatedly interrupt your interviewee to comment on his or her comments; remember you are there to hear his or her responses to your questions.

3. Don't interview your teacher in the teachers' lounge or any other public space in the school. (You run the risk of too many interruptions.)

4. Don't ask questions that could be perceived as rude, pushy, or offensive. Examples of such questions include:

   (a) Do you get along with the principal of your school? Or worse: Do you like the principal of your school?

   (b) How much money does a teacher with your experience make? (You can find this out at the school-district office by asking for the district salary schedule.)

   (c) Why does this school have such a drab environment?

   (d) Doesn't the low status of the teaching profession bother you?

   (e) All I see are older teachers in this school. Don't they hire young teachers in this district?

   (f) The kids in this school really look messy. Does that affect their school work?

Please note that the preceding questions (a–f) ask about things that are natural for you to be curious about. *But,* on your first or second visit these questions would be unnatural and inappropriate for a relative stranger to ask. We mention the second visit because we have learned that structured interviews can easily lead to a follow-up observation and a second interview. When the interview has gone well, the interviewer simply says to the teacher: "You know, Mrs. Sanchez, I really enjoyed today's interview and learned quite a bit; do you think I could possibly spend some time observing in your class?" A semistructured interview would likely follow the observation.

At this point, you should be feeling more confident about carrying out a structured interview with a teacher. You have a clear idea about what a structured interview is, how to develop one, and how to use an interview rationale to get your interview. You have also learned about the concern that a teacher-education program might have about its image, and your responsibilities to that program and your own future. We will now discuss several other important interview-related questions:

1. How do you decide exactly whom to call for an interview?
2. Once the interview has been arranged, how do you organize yourself for data collection and data analysis?
3. What do you do with the set of interview data that results from your several or more interviews?

Whom Do You Interview?

This fundamentally important question leads one to ask: Why not go out and interview any teacher who is willing to be interviewed? Indeed, there would be some wisdom in doing this. But there is too much variety in our profession to opt for this strategy. Our experience suggests that the teachers who can best help prospective teachers decide whether or not the career of teaching is the right one for them are teachers who have experienced success in their careers. Thus, we recommend that the teachers whom you contact be ones who have been selected by the professors in your teacher-education program, or ones recommended by these selected teachers.

Collecting and Organizing Your Data

To collect data during and after your interview, we recommend that you employ the "key word—scribble—download" strategy. This strategy involves:

1. Typing up or handwriting your questions into an interview schedule and leaving 3 or 4 inches of space between each of the questions (the interview schedule is your sequenced, refined list of questions), and then making a xeroxed copy of your schedule. Thus, you go into your interview with *two* copies of your interview schedule.
2. Using your first copy of the interview schedule to copy or scribble down key words or phrases from the teacher's responses for each question, while maintaining ongoing eye contact with the teacher (a neat trick and something you'll get better at).
3. Using your key words and phrases and your second copy of the inter-

view schedule to write down your thoughts immediately or soon after (within an hour of) the interview. During this "downloading" phase, you will use your key words and memory to write up a more complete, extended description of the teacher's reply to each question. These extended descriptions provide the data for the analysis and synthesis described below.

4. Read what you have just written in Step 3, and on the same or a separate sheet, list any new questions that stem from data in your notes.

Data Analysis and Synthesis

Data analysis is something you should do for each individual interview, as well as something that should occur when the notes from several interviews have accumulated.

To begin with, a day or two after each individual interview, you should examine your extended notes to see if you have anything to add to them. Occasionally, you will remember something 48 hours after the interview that was overlooked during the downloading, and sometimes you will see something new in your notes that leads to a new awareness about what your teacher meant with a certain remark. The examination might also suggest new questions for a second interview with the same teacher, perhaps following from an arranged observation, or the questions might be used with a revised interview schedule for a new teacher.

At a later point, when you have the extended notes from several interviews, a different type of analysis will be appropriate. At that point, you will be in a position to compare, contrast, and make inferences based on the data you have collected. After you have reread all your interview notes and made mental notes of the points of similarity and contrast, it would be fruitful to answer the following question in your mind *and* on paper:

> From these interviews, and (perhaps) follow-up observations, what have I (tentatively) learned or decided about teaching and the teaching profession?

Your written response to this question will be your data synthesis, and it will help you extract from the interview data the knowledge that will inform and influence your later observations, interviews, and decisions about a career in teaching. Some of these thoughts should be explored in greater depth in your journal notes.

Activities for Chapter Five

Since the focus of this chapter was on the design and implementation of semistructured interviews, all of the activities spelled out will involve you in that type of interview. The activities we have selected, and their organization, assume two things: first, that some of you will be assigned to one main cooperating teacher during your early field experience, and, second, that the interview with your assigned teacher will be most fruitful if carried out in the middle or toward the end of the quarter or semester. At the same time, we encourage you to design and carry out semistructured interviews as soon as possible; your classmates, professors, and student teachers in your program, and even your spouse can help you sharpen your interviewing skills.

Core Activity
The Semistructured Interview

Design and conduct a semistructured interview with your cooperating teacher, or a veteran teacher (8 to 25 years of experience) if you have not been assigned to a cooperating teacher during your early field-experience course. Use the key word—scribble—download strategy to develop a data base from each interview. When the data base is established, analyze your data to answer this question:

> From the actual interview, and my analysis of the data generated by the interview, what have I learned about teaching and/or the teaching profession?

Suggested Activity One
The Experienced Teacher

Repeat the core activity; however, this time interview teachers who have been teaching for two to five years. After responding to the "What have I learned about teaching or the teaching profession?" question, compare and contrast the responses of the veteran and new teachers.

Suggested Activity Two
The Award-Winning Teacher

Design and conduct a semistructured interview with an award-winning teacher, possibly the county or school-district teacher-of-the-year. This interview should be conducted by two members of your class in front of the whole class, and could be videotaped by the instructor for later use.

Suggested Activity Three
The University Instructor

Design and conduct a semistructured interview with one of your favorite university instructors. During your interview (and observation) of this instructor, try to identify, and then describe, the elements of this instructor's teaching style that seem most significant to you. If you choose this activity, the following questions may prove helpful to you:

1. What characteristics, or behaviors, combine to make this instructor so successful?
2. What characteristics make this instructor a special, almost unique, instructor?
3. Which aspects of this instructor's teaching style, or behavioral performance, appear to be artistic, or artful, in nature?

Suggested Activity Four
The Teacher Candidate

Design and conduct a semistructured interview with a classmate or student teacher (preferably a friend). It is likely that you will compose a set of original questions for this interview because the questions enumerated earlier in this chapter do not apply. The major purpose of Activity Four, beyond gathering useful information, is to practice interviewing. Therefore, audiotaping and then listening to your interview may prove helpful. Keep in mind that Activity Four is the only interview in which we recommend using a tape recorder.

Suggested Activity Five
Your Favorite Teacher

If possible, design and conduct an interview with one of your favorite K–12 teachers. Beyond the usual revealing information derived, this interview might be a nice way to say "thank you" to a teacher who probably influenced your own decision to become a teacher.

Suggested Activity Six
The Typical Teacher's Day

Now that you've had the opportunity to orient yourself physically within the school building and classroom, you will find it helpful to orient yourself to a typical day in the life of a teacher. Although most teachers would argue that none of their days are typical, careful observation and some well-stated questions should give you a reasonably clear picture of how your cooperating teacher spends his or her time.

The core of the teacher's daily activities will be the courses or content areas he or she teaches. Using those as the cornerstones of your teacher's daily time grid, complete the grid on the next page by questioning the teacher about the following:

1. What time does the teacher usually arrive at school?

2. What kinds of activities does the teacher engage in between arriving at school and the beginning of classes? Any special duties or regularly scheduled meetings?

3. How is the teacher's time spent between classes and/or during free periods, lunch, recess, and so on?

4. During class time, is the teacher constantly directing instruction or are free* times built into the teaching schedule?

5. Have the teacher estimate the percentage of his or her daily time that is spent doing noninstructional activities (i.e., bus duty, lunchroom duty, administrative paperwork, calling parents, collecting money, checking attendance, etc.).

6. How much time does the teacher spend in the building after school? Is that by choice? What activities usually take up after-school time?

7. What extracurricular activities is the teacher in charge of? How much time does that take per day?

8. Have the teacher estimate the total number of hours he or she spends per day in school-related activities.

---

*Free times could be segments of time where students do seat work and the teacher grades papers or handles routine administrative paperwork.

The Teacher's Day

On the grid below, indicate the predominant activities during the teacher's waking hours. In the space provided, indicate the duration of the activity and whether it was school-related or nonschool-related time.

Time	Description of Activity	Duration	School-Related	Nonschool-Related
6:00 a.m. to 7:00 a.m.				
to 8:00 a.m.				
to 9:00 a.m.				
to 10:00 a.m.				
to 11:00 a.m.				
to noon				
to 1:00 p.m.				
to 2:00 p.m.				
to 3:00 p.m.				
to 4:00 p.m.				
to 5:00 p.m.				
to 6:00 p.m.				
to 7:00 p.m.				
to 8:00 p.m.				
to 9:00 p.m.				
to 10:00 p.m.				
to 11:00 p.m.				
to midnight				

Tabulate the Following:

1. Total number of hours in teacher's typical work day. _____

2. Percentage of time spent in school-related activities. _____ %

3. Percentage of time spent in nonschool-related activities. _____ %

4. Percentage of school-related activities that are noninstructional. _____ %

5. Total number of hours spent teaching or performing instructionally related activities (setting up labs, learning centers, etc.). _____ %

Although the general impression of the public is that teachers work from 8:30 a.m. to 3:30 p.m. and have June, July, and August for vacation time, nothing could be further from the truth. Teachers' days are usually long and their schedules rarely allow much time for relaxation, regrouping, and regeneration. During the day, relaxation time consists mainly of stolen moments as even free periods are consumed with class preparation, grading papers, or calling parents. In addition, the three months' vacation in summer is usually spent either taking additional graduate coursework or supplementing the yearly income or, in some cases, both.

To fully appreciate the rigors of teaching, one must analyze the amount of time spent doing school-related activities and the physical and emotional effects on the individual due to the intensive nature of that time. Introducing yourself to schools and teaching requires a thorough assessment of the environments in which teaching occurs and conditions under which teachers perform their daily teaching and nonteaching routines. Even a cursory analysis provides convincing evidence that a considerable gap exists between the general impressions of the public and the realities of the teaching profession.

Student Name _____   Date _____

Journal Entry

Inasmuch as this chapter focused on interviewing classroom teachers, your journal entry should comment or elaborate on:

1. What you learned from the set of interviews you conducted; and
2. Your thoughts about interviewing as a research strategy. Was it a strategy that worked for you, or did you find it difficult to gather information in the face-to-face mode? What did you like about the interviewing process? What, if anything, would you do differently in your next interview?

_____

_____

_____

_____

_____

_____

_____

_____

_____

_____

_____

_____

_____

_____

_____

_____

Questions for Discussion

1. For a variety of reasons, in the past as well as the present, the teaching profession has had an extremely high turnover rate. When you consider your future in teaching, do you perceive yourself as someone who will become a veteran teacher?

2. In the next chapter on "The Teacher's Image" it is noted that the public has not always viewed teaching and the teaching profession in a positive light. Given the data derived from the interviews in this chapter, and the observations and interviews conducted in previous chapters, what is your view of the teaching profession? More specifically:

   (a) Do you consider teaching to be a profession? If yes, why? If not, why not?

   (b) Do you believe that teaching is a profession or career that you will find satisfying and be able to take pride in? Why? Why not?

3. The teachers you interviewed had the opportunity to discuss changes that might occur in the role of teacher in the next five years. Comment on the responses made by the teachers, and then ask the instructor of your course the same question.

4. Where and how do you think interviewing might fit into your approach to teaching?

References

DeVito, J. A. (1986). *The interpersonal communication book.* New York: Harper & Row.

Gordon, R. (1980). *Interviewing: Strategy, techniques, and tactics.* Homewood, Ill: The Dorsey Press.

Kahn, R. L., & Cannell, C. F. (1982). *The dynamics of interviewing.* New York: John Wiley & Sons.

Steil, L. K., Barker, L. L., & Watson, K. W. (1983). *Effective listening.* Reading, Mass.: Addison-Wesley.

Stewart, C. J., & Cash, W. B., Jr. (1988). *Interviewing: Principles and practices* (5th edition). Dubuque, Iowa: Wm. C. Brown.

Wilmot, W. W. (1987). *Dyadic communication.* New York: Random House/Alfred Knopf.

Images of the Teacher

Up to this point, you've been directing your observations and your thinking toward the school and the people who work in it. You've begun the process of examining what occurs in school buildings and classrooms and why some schools seem to be more successful than others in reaching their goals. Since your primary purpose is to discover if you want to become a teacher, however, the role or image of the teacher in the school is of critical importance. The focus in this chapter is on the teacher, or rather the image of the teacher, and how that image has affected your perception of the teaching profession. You may be surprised to discover that the image of teachers you've come to accept is a function of both your own experience in schools and the depiction of teachers by others who influence you in conscious and unconscious ways.

Because of these influences, your decision to enter teaching will be shaped by this combination of experiences in school and by images of teachers presented in books, newspapers, movies, and television. Teachers, like doctors and lawyers, are often inviting targets for media stereotypes. Doctors and lawyers, however, unlike teachers, are often presented as dedicated professionals employing considerable intelligence and/or occasional wit in solving the perplexing problems of their professions with the latest practices and technologies. Rarely are teachers shown as doing more than handling problem students or unsympathetic administrators.* While television viewers are frequently provided with insights into the courtroom practices of talented lawyers and the operating-room techniques of skilled surgeons, teachers are usually depicted employing the most traditional methodologies (lectures/discussion) to students who are generally eager for learning during periods of somewhere around five minutes. Not surprisingly, teaching usually looks easy under those conditions. Only recently have the media begun to portray teachers in realistic and more positive roles.

---

*Principals are almost always presented unsympathetically as autocratic pencil pushers wrapped up in maintaining the bureaucracy at all costs. In that sense, they usually look worse than the teachers.

What of these images? To what extent do they influence our perceptions of teachers and teaching? How accurate are they? What impact have they had on those teachers currently in the profession? The answers to some of these questions, of course, will lie within the context of your observations and interviews with teachers. Others, however, exist within you as you have had your perceptions shaped, molded and "massaged" by the media. In the next section, we'll explore how some of these images have been created by various media and then gauge your reaction to the degree to which these images influenced or did not influence you. Then you'll pose some of these same questions to classroom teachers to determine how much they see of themselves and others in these images.

The Teacher in Literature, Film, and Television

From Washington Irving's characterization of Ichabod Crane as a hapless pedagog immersed in his own self-importance and fears to Mark Twain's depiction of the one-room schoolmaster who sneaks a peek at Gray's *Anatomy* and has his "dome gilded" (his bald head painted gold) by Tom Sawyer and has friends, up to the more sympathetic, two-dimensional view of the young, but obviously misguided, progressive elementary teacher in Harper Lee's *To Kill a Mockingbird,* the treatment of teachers in literature has only occasionally been positive.

Female teachers in literature are often depicted as unattractive physically, undesirable sexually, and unskilled socially. The "schoolmarm" image remains the dominant perspective of many writers. Male teachers fare little better although they are occasionally shown as having lustful yearnings for a two-dimensional female character. These yearnings, however, inevitably lead to the teacher's downfall in the community. The literary message is clear. Teachers are ordinary-looking, asexual, moderately intelligent (though often in an eccentric way), socially inept public servants. Their ambitions are minimal and limited primarily toward salvaging some recalcitrant student(s). Females are teaching only until they can find a suitable mate, or, because of a jilted love, until they become schoolmarmish spinsters. More recently, however, novels by Judy Blume and others have presented teachers in a realistic, positive light and these literary images may have affected your perceptions of teaching.

Research on Hollywood films over the past 50 years suggests that teachers have fared as poorly in that medium as they have in literature. Teachers in films made before the 1970s are frequently shown as pedantic, dull, and sometimes cruel to their students. Even when teachers are depicted as sympathetic to the needs of adolescents, they are also shown as being confused by the actions of young people and dismayed by the differences in the basic values held by the students and themselves. It appears in numerous cases that the teachers have had little formal training in psychology, pedagogy, and philosophy and have literally stepped in front of the class with little more than the force of their personalities to see them through.

Even when teachers are depicted in a generally positive light in books and in films such as Sidney Poitier in *To Sir with Love,* Nick Nolte in *Teachers,* and William Hurt in *Children of a Lesser God,* they are shown as struggling against enormous odds and at great personal cost. Teachers, it appears, must either be social misfits or super heroes. These are images that can create an unrealistic view of education and teaching particularly when contrasted with the realities of classroom life in most schools. Rarely does one find a Mr. Chips or a Miss Dove or a Miss Jean Brodie in elementary or secondary classrooms and schools. When portrayed as larger than life on film, characters like Mr. Chips have a way of blending with our actual experiences in schools to create a curious mixture of fantasy and reality in our unconscious. Because of the prolonged and frequently intense nature of our school experiences, as opposed to our limited experience with doctors and lawyers, film images can have a powerful effect on our recollection of teachers in a manner that is unlike our recollection of any other profession.

Television images have an impact on perceptions that frequently exceed those of film. Films depict memorable people while television depicts memorable characters. In the 1950s, teachers were seen as comedic individuals who had to maintain their resolute calmness when faced with the light-hearted antics of their students. In the 1960s and early 1970s, the serious-minded, student-centered teachers such as Mr. Novak or Pete Dixon in television's "Room 222" appeared on the school scene to guide their frequently troubled charges through adolescence. Although sometimes humorous, these teachers were never comedic. This was also a period in which more individuals were drawn into teaching than ever before or since.

The late 1970s ushered in the teacher as stand-up comedian when the Sweathogs welcomed back Kotter (Gabe Kaplan). Here, the teacher was totally immersed in the lives of his students and they in his. This, of course, was because he had been "one of them," proving that in teaching, unlike any other profession, you can go home again. Although essentially a situation comedy and vehicle for Gabe Kaplan, the image of teacher portrayed in this popular series was caring, clever, and on the whole, serious and positive. Kotter's positive teacher image is in the same vein as the hardworking, intelligent teacher images of "Room 222" and the generally positive images presented in the New York City–based television series "Fame." Recent comedy and dramatic series have continued this more positive trend toward teachers and, to some extent, administrators. In "Head of the Class," a nomadic substitute teacher is drawn into a class of gifted students. He is shown as student-centered, comic-serious and thoroughly dedicated to his gifted "sweathogs." Similarly, in the "Bronx Zoo," teachers, and particularly the principal, struggle against some enormous problems in order to make school a positive experience for students. As might be expected in any large high school, the teachers cover a range of attitudes, skills, and levels of dedication to the task.

Thus, while we have seen an uneven progression toward more serious, mature teachers in school-based books, movies, and television series in the past 10 years, on the whole, the images of teachers created by the media still leave much to be desired in terms of authenticity, depth, and variety. Because many adults grew up with the older, more distorted images of teachers and teaching, their perceptions of schools might be different than yours. Frequently, these more distorted images have found their way into the news media.

Schools, Teachers, and News Images

In recent years, schools and the teaching profession have come under fire by the news media and politicians more extensively than ever before. Much of this, of course, can be attributed to a general demystification of all institutions in American society that occurred in the 1960s and 1970s, but nonetheless, the criticisms have resulted in a serious erosion of the public image of teachers and teaching.

To what extent are these criticisms valid and what effect have they had on teachers' self-images? Do these emerging images accurately depict the conditions of schools and the skills of teachers? To what degree are the statements about teachers and teaching enumerated in the Core Activity actually reflections of schools that the critics recall from their own childhood rather than schools of the 1980s? Why do local papers in small towns frequently present positive views of the schools in contrast to the national news? Which perspective is more accurate?

Core Activity

News Images of Education

Following are listed some statements that have appeared in or on one or more of the media that impact on you every day. After each statement, indicate whether you believe the assertion is true or false and give a reason for your choice. (Sample responses to each item can be found later in this core activity.)

1. Teaching attracts the less capable college students. Scholastic Aptitude Test (SAT) scores of education majors are among the lowest of any majors on college campuses.

True   False

Reason: _____

_____

_____

_____

_____

2. The teaching field has a distressingly high percentage of teachers who have difficulty writing intelligent sentences or even spelling simple words correctly.

                    True   False

Reason: _____

        _____

        _____

        _____

        _____

3. Schools are about to be overwhelmed by a "rising tide of mediocrity" because of, among other things, an intellectually weak curriculum and poor teaching.

                    True   False

Reason: _____

        _____

        _____

        _____

        _____

4. Schools are doing only marginally better in teaching reading since 1978, but writing skills continue to decline in *all* age groups.

                    True   False

Reason: _____

        _____

        _____

        _____

        _____

5. After nearly 20 years of steady decline in the SAT scores of high-school graduates, a small, statistically insignificant increase was found in the past three years.

True   False

Reason: _____

_____

_____

_____

_____

6. Secondary teachers have reached a "compromise" with their students. In essence, teachers will lower their expectations and demands if students behave in a reasonable manner.

True   False

Reason: _____

_____

_____

_____

_____

7. American students lag behind virtually every other industrialized nation in math and science achievement-test scores even when our best students are compared with the best students of other countries.

True   False

Reason: _____

_____

_____

_____

_____

8. The number of private parochial and nonsectarian schools has risen dramatically over the past 10 years nationwide. The number of parents seeking to educate their children at home has increased simultaneously. Both figures reflect a growing dissatisfaction with the quality and focus of education in public schools.

True   False

Reason: _____

_____

_____

_____

_____

While your responses may not totally agree with the reasons given on the following pages, these sample responses reflect sentiments that have been given wide play in the news media and have created a public image of teachers and schools that is difficult to overcome. Indeed, some practicing teachers share these images themselves. Already, you may have been approached by a teacher who is a family friend, or who is a teacher in the school where you're observing. Sometimes these teachers will question your decision to enter teaching. They might even suggest that you reconsider your decision because they would not have entered teaching if they had it to do over again.

Are the teachers you are observing well respected by students, parents, and others?

"I would appreciate it very much if you wouldn't hum the tune from 'The Twilight Zone' every time I enter the classroom!"

originally published in Phi Delta Kappan

By now you may have concluded that the teacher's image is shaky both within the profession and nationally. While there is some validity to that conclusion, it doesn't mean that image equates with substance because there are more positives in the image than are generally recognized. Therefore, part of your growth as a teacher will involve confronting the issues of image versus substance, myth versus reality, and opinion versus fact. In the following activities, you will explore the nature of the teacher image and its effect on teaching and schools. From your explorations, you will draw conclusions supported by facts, realities, and substance. This will enable you to discover that society is deeply indebted to teachers and many teachers feel good about their decision to enter teaching. Along the way you may recollect a teacher you had who helped you out when you were upset or in a personal crisis. You may also find that teachers have many sources of joy as well as frustration. Finally, you may learn that part of the challenge of becoming a teacher is learning to be yourself rather than fitting or overcoming an image that is neither accurate nor real.

Sample Responses and Supporting Reasons

At the beginning of this Core Activity you responded to some statements that have appeared recently in the media. We have summarized a few arguments on both sides of the issue that have been presented in various sources. The responses you wrote may be similar to the ones that follow, but if they're not, you may want to analyze and discuss the points of divergence with other students in your class. Be particularly conscious of conclusions based on false assumptions and/or poor research techniques.

1. *True:*
    The SAT scores of intended education majors were lower than those of almost every other intended major in 1973 and these scores continued to fall faster than the declining national average until 1983. Even though the gap between the national average and the scores of education majors is being narrowed, the SAT scores of those intending to major in education fall below the state's average SAT score in all 50 states and the District of Columbia.
    False:
    The SAT scores of high-school students who say they intend to major in education when they get to college are rising faster than the national average. The once wide gap between the national average and the intended education majors' average has narrowed from 80 points in 1982 to 70 points in 1985. Within that same time period the gap for verbal SAT scores is 27 points less, and for math scores the gap is 43 points less.

2. *True:*
    The low SAT scores that teachers achieve show that many may be lacking in skills necessary to teach the writing of clear, intelligent sentences and basic spelling skills. One of the reasons for this outrageous condition is that many teacher-training institutions do not ever consider SAT or Amer-

ican College Testing (ACT) scores when considering whether or not to admit a student to the program. Rarely does anyone who applies for admission into a teacher-education program get rejected. Most of the institutions don't even keep any high-school information about their teacher-education students. Therefore, many prospective teachers can get into a program and even obtain a degree and certification without possessing basic writing and spelling skills.

False:

With more and more schools requiring teaching candidates to demonstrate academic and professional competencies by some type of instrument—National Teacher's Examination (NTE) or Pre-professional Skills Test (PPST) for example—it is becoming very difficult to obtain a teaching position if one cannot read, write, or spell adequately. As of this date, there is no really hard data that has been presented concerning the academic caliber of persons who go through the process of becoming teachers. Therefore, any evidence presenting new teachers as not being competent is purely circumstantial.

3. *True:*

Secondary-school curricula have been homogenized, diluted, and diffused to the point that they no longer have a central purpose. Because of this lack of direction, more and more students are taking a general program of study instead of vocational or college-preparatory programs. Twenty-five percent of the credits earned by students who are enrolled in the general track are in physical and health education, work experience outside of school, remedial English and mathematics, and personal service and development courses, such as training for adulthood and marriage.

Too many teachers are coming from the lower 25 percent of high-school and college students. In many teacher-training institutions, the courses are geared heavily toward educational-methods courses instead of subjects to be taught. Upon entering college, many of the candidates best-qualified to teach do not choose to do so because the average salary is so low in comparison to other majors. Finally, many newly employed teachers are forced to teach outside their subject areas due to shortages in subjects such as science, mathematics, and English.

False:

By offering a wide range of curricular opportunities, we are allowing students the choice of direction for themselves. In this sense, the teacher is a coach, or helper, instead of a teller. By doing this, we also give adolescents the chance to explore different avenues and find out who they are, what they like or dislike, and what direction they might want to see their future take. By allowing freedom of choice, schools are also modeling a principle of democracy that is unique when compared to the education systems of other nations.

Although the average salary for teachers is still low when compared to other professions, the tide is beginning to turn. Salaries are beginning to rise at a slow but fairly steady pace. With the implementation of the NTE or PPST examination for teachers, many schools are only looking for candidates who score well on these tests. Those who accomplish this tend to be above the lower 25 percent of graduating students. Finally, more and more teachers are graduating today who are certified in shortage areas such as English, mathematics, and science.

4. *True:*

In business situations such as filling out an information form, writing skills of most American students are inadequate. At age 9, only three out of every 20 students could correctly accomplish this goal. At age 13, five out of every 20; at age 17, 12 out of every 20; and finally only 10 out of every 20 adults could correctly fill out a basic information form. Generally, the level of writing skills shown nationally is not very high. By age 9, few individuals have mastered the basics of written English; by age 17, about one-half of the individuals have some mastery of the basics, but they rarely attempt anything beyond the simplest constructions or use anything beyond a rather limited vocabulary. At no age level do individuals show much of a flair for writing.

False:

Studies have shown that the general writing ability of Americans increases with age. This is illustrated by the ability to write an informative note. Although the numbers show only a small portion of students are demonstrating adequate skills, they do negate the assertion that writing skills are continuing to decline. Three out of every 10 students who were 9 years old could write an informative note that was acceptable. Seven out of every 10 students at age 13 could do it, and eight out of every 10 students aged 17 could accomplish this.

The assertion also states that teaching reading skills is getting only marginally better. However, according to the *National Assessment of Educational Progress* (1987) this is not so. "The vast majority of young Americans can read fairly simple material, but many cannot: many young Americans are handicapped by deficient reading skills. They cannot follow simple directions, and they find it difficult to draw inferences or conclusions based on what they do understand when they read."

5. *True:*

Between the years of 1982 and 1985, SAT scores for education majors began to climb once again. In 1982, the national average SAT score was 893 and the intended education majors score was 813—80 points under the national average. In 1985, the average SAT score rose to 906 for the national average and to 836 for intended majors in education, thus narrowing the gap slightly to 70 points. With this information in mind one can conclude that the scores for prospective teachers are rising, but at a slow rate.

False:

Although the average scores for future education majors are increasing, the average national score is likewise growing at a similar pace. Therefore, even despite the increase, it remains true that in all 50 states and the District of Columbia, the SAT scores of those intending to major in education are still far below the average. Finally, the scores obtained by education majors are still the lowest of all other majors.

6. *True:*

Such compromise as described in the assertion is necessary in many schools today because it is impossible for teachers and students to sustain rigorous, adventurous activity over a full six-hour day. By doing this, many adolescents and students who probably would not get any education are at least getting the bare minimum by agreeing to this type of learning environment.

False:

If effective learning is to take place, both the student and the teacher must agree on the objectives to be met and the means that will be used to meet them. The students must trust the teacher and must be informed of what is expected of them and why, what the standards are and why, and how to behave, both in school and on the job. When this is done, students will know where the teacher stands and that there are limits to their behavior. Thus, a learning environment can be created that will help them the most. By doing this, the teacher is letting the students know that he or she cares about them by setting standards that will help students to grow and therefore influence their futures.

7. *True:*

Even when comparing math scores of equal proportions of age groups, U.S. students are still lagging behind many countries such as Israel, England, France, Japan, and Sweden. The United States is also behind students of other nations in science. When comparing mean science scores of the top 5 percent of students, the United States is lagging behind such nations as New Zealand, England, Australia, Scotland, Sweden, and Hungary.

False:

Although only the elite in many other nations get to continue their education at the secondary level (high school), they do not differ considerably from the high-school elite in the United States. It is also unfair to make cross-cultural comparisons between nations who have different educational systems.

Even though the United States may be behind several countries in mean science scores, the science scores of the top 5 percent of its students are higher than those of the industrialized nations of West Germany and France.

8. *True:*

In 1985, a study by Hoffer, Greeley, and Coleman concluded that Catholic schools were more effective than public schools in fostering academic achievement. This study was a follow-up to substantiate the Coleman, Hoffer, and Kilgore study of 1982 that also showed achievement is greater in Catholic and private schools than in the public schools.

False:

Several other studies have concluded that there is little evidence that private nonsectarian schools produce better student performance than public schools in tests of mathematics and reading achievement. Even though research shows that Catholic high-school students were estimated to have learned slightly more than did students in public schools, these effects were short-term ones and, therefore, cannot be taken seriously. This has been proven by research that shows that in the long-term, Catholic-school students do no better than public-school students in vocabulary and actually do worse in math.

Suggested Activity One
Teachers' Images

As you were directly experiencing teachers and schools during your childhood and adolescence, you were probably influenced considerably through your interactions with these teachers or with family friends who were (are) teachers. In addition, you were exposed to a variety of media models on television and in movies and books. These models also had an influence on your perceptions of teachers and teaching. In the spaces below, describe the characteristics and behaviors (positive and negative) of these teachers and the media models you were exposed to, and briefly discuss how your perceptions of teachers and teaching were influenced. Please note that your influential teacher could be a media figure like Mr. Dixon, or Kotter, or could be a real teacher whom you experienced in your own school career.

My Most Influential Teacher(s)

The Teacher I Would Most Like to Emulate

Characteristics:

Behaviors:

The Teacher(s) I Would Least Like to Emulate

Characteristics:

Behaviors:

Suggested Activity Two
Media Role Models

Media Role Models That Influenced My Perceptions of Teachers and Teaching

---

Briefly discuss how your ideas about teaching were influenced by the characteristics listed below.

1. Movie Roles:
   Male

   Female

2. Television Roles:
   Male

   Female

3. Literary Roles:
   Male

Female

Suggested Activity Three

How Does Your Teacher Feel About Teaching?

In the previous activity, you were asked to examine your own images of teachers and teaching, some of which were derived from direct experiences and some from media models. In this activity, you will continue to apply your interviewing skills in a structured interview with the teacher you're observing and other teachers with whom you may have contact. Besides the questions suggested below, feel free to incorporate some items of your own based upon your observations and class discussions.

Questions for Classroom Teachers

1. Were there any teachers that you had in school who influenced your decision to enter teaching? In what ways did they influence you?

2. Were there any behaviors or characteristics of these teachers that you sought to emulate when you entered teaching? What were some examples of these behaviors or characteristics?

3. What do you perceive to be the public image of teachers in American society today? Is this image accurate or misleading? In what ways?

4. Do movies, television, and novels depict teachers accurately or stereotypically?

5. Are there media role models of teachers that you found to be particularly gratifying (e.g., Sidney Poitier, Kotter, Mr. Chips, William Hurt)?

6. Are there media role models of teachers that you found to be particularly disheartening (e.g., the study hall supervisor in the movie "Breakfast Club," Ichabod Crane, Mr. Peepers)?

7. How do the local papers contribute to your community's perception of local teachers? Do they portray teachers in a positive light?

8. Do you feel you have to maintain one image in school and/or with parents and another image in your private life? Does that create any difficulties for you?

9. In what ways has the teacher's image changed since you began teaching? What are your feelings about those changes?

Additional questions . . .

From your data, what conclusions can you draw about working teachers' perceptions of teacher image?

How do these perceptions compare to your own?

Student Name _____   Date _____

Journal Entry

Since this chapter concentrated on teacher image and how that image has evolved, your journal entry for this chapter should concentrate on your perceptions of teachers and teaching and how you arrived at your perceptions. Within this journal entry, you should elaborate on the feelings you had when you:

1. Interviewed teachers on their perceptions of teacher image.
2. Considered the role media play in shaping your image and the public's image of teachers.
3. Listened to your class discuss their findings relative to recent criticisms of teachers and schools.
4. Reflected on your own decision to enter teaching and the kind of public image you would like to create as a teacher.

_____

_____

_____

_____

_____

_____

_____

_____

_____

_____

_____

_____

_____

_____

Questions for Discussion

1. How critical is the public's image of teachers and teaching to your decision to enter teaching?

2. How could teachers effectively improve their image with the public? Suggest some strategies that school districts, teacher organizations, or student-teacher groups might employ to attain these goals.

3. Some critics have suggested that teachers create two images—one that reflects their public selves and another that reflects their private selves. Based on your observations, interviews, and class discussions analyze the extent to which teachers do sustain two distinct images.

4. Given your analyses of the media models of teachers, discuss how these models create stereotypes of the teaching profession and how they may create public expectations that are difficult for teachers to attain.

5. Describe your ideal teacher and the sources (real teachers, media models, etc.) that you drew upon to create this image.

References

Cohn, M. M., R. B. Kottkamp and E. F. Provenzo, Jr. (1987). *To be a teacher.* Random House, New York. 14–20.

Coleman, J. S., T. Hoffer and S. Kilgore. (1982, April). Achievement and segregation in secondary schools: A look at public and private school differences. *Sociology of Education.* 55:162–182.

Feistritzer, E. C. (1985). The condition of teaching: A state by state analysis. A Carnegie Foundation technical report. Carnegie Foundation for the advancement of teaching, 172 pages. Princeton, N.J. 69–72, 92–95.

Hoffer, T., A. Greeley and J. S. Coleman. (1985, April). Achievement growth in public and Catholic schools. *Sociology of Education.* 58:74–97.

Husen, T. (1983, March). Are standards in U.S. schools really lagging behind those in other countries? *Phi Delta Kappan,* 455–461.

Johnson, S. S. (1987). Update on education: A digest of the national assessment of educational progress. Education Commission of the States, Denver, Colorado.

National Commission on Excellence in Education. (1983). *A nation at risk: The imperative for school reform.* Washington, D.C.

Sizer, T. (1984). *Horace's compromise: The dilemma of the American high school.* Boston: Houghton Mifflin.

Williams, D. A. (1985, September). Why teachers fail. *Newsweek,* 64–66.

Wolfle, L. M. (1987, May). Enduring cognitive effects of public and private schools. *Educational Researcher,* 5–10.

CHAPTER 7

The School and Its Community

Once upon a time, there were no schools. One learned everything from one's family or tribe or from the hard lessons of direct experience. Most of what was to be learned was survival skills: how to hunt and trap, how to keep the fire going, and how to find good water. The poor learners usually had short lives, both individually and as communities. Experience was, indeed, a harsh teacher.

As time progressed, some tribal communities developed more and more skills and had more and more to pass on to the young. Increasingly, it seemed inefficient for everyone to do everything. Also, it became clear that people had different talents, and different contributions to make to the welfare of the community. Some could build; some could hunt; some could lead. The human community discovered the specialization of labor. The accumulation of knowledge and skills plus the specialization of labor is tightly linked to the history of education. At a certain point in the evolution of a human community, it became inefficient for parents to spend so much time teaching their children. The story of the education of Alexander the Great is a good example. Alexander's father, Philip of Macedon, was too busy ruling and extending his empire to teach his son all that Philip knew Alexander would need to know to follow in his footsteps, so he hired the wisest man in the then known world to teach his son. He hired Aristotle, and the great Greek philosopher became the personal tutor of the young man who was to conquer and rule all of the then known world.

But as the example suggests, formal education was a luxury, something reserved for the elite. In the Roman Empire, wealthy families often had teachers who were slaves, captured from far-off lands. Later, the Church began schools, usually attached to monasteries. These often evolved into universities, where knowledge was collected, copied, codified, and passed on. Royal courts began to hire teachers. Later, the wealthy merchant classes hired tutors, and they established small schools for their children. But in all of these examples, schooling was by and large something of a social luxury, and something reserved for those who would eventually lead the community in some way: as a ruler, as a churchman, as a merchant, or, in order to continue the line, as a scholar-teacher. Schools, then, served the social elite of a community and, only indirectly, the rest of the community.

Schooling was a major factor in the development of the New World. In colonial New England, Puritan parents believed that it was important for children to be able to read the Bible and, thus, protect themselves from Satan. On the other hand, they were too busy eking out a living from the cold, rocky soil of New England to teach them themselves. They decided on the establishment of schools and, in 1647, passed the Old Deluder Act. This historic act set the pattern for community-supported schools. It required that every town of 50 or more families pay a man to teach the children to read and write. From these beginnings, schools spread across and down the continent. As knowledge and skills developed and as the demands of commerce and an ever more complex business world emerged, schools snowballed. Instead of education being the province of the rulers and the wealthy, it was spread to everyone. More and more children began to go to school for longer and longer periods of time. Grades and levels of schooling were established. Grammar schools were followed by high schools.

Following the pattern set in New England, communities saw that it was in their best interest to require education. So education became compulsory and it continued to require more and more time from the lives of children and youth. Also, the specialization of labor that originally led to the selection of certain people to be teachers (to be, in effect, culture carriers) led to increasing specialization among teachers. As communities wanted more and more to be taught, it became clear that specialization was needed *within* teaching, so elementary teachers were educated who specialized in the primary grades and physics teachers were trained for the more advanced students and so on. Both these trends, toward more education for more people and more specialization within teaching, have continued into the present, and, no doubt, will increase in the future.

Schools, then, have developed as a direct result of community needs and sometimes demands. As such, they reflect what a community believes the community needs to survive. In times of rapid social and technological changes, like the present, schools represent what people think their children will need to live successful lives and maintain the community in the future. And, different communities make different choices. The Amish communities in the Midwest have rejected much of twentieth-century technological progress and its values. As a result, their schools teach the Bible and the basics and shun most literature, science, mathematics, and vocational programs that make up much of the curriculum in modern schools.

One of the most distinctive features of the American system of education is the relationship between schools and their communities. For one thing, we have a highly decentralized school system, which allows a local community to have an enormous range of choice in how they wish to structure school and what they want to teach their children. Most modern nations, like Russia and France, on the other hand, are centralized. What the minister of education in Moscow or Paris says about what will be taught in the third grade or in the eleventh grade will be taught throughout the country. The minister of education, in effect, represents all the people and one set of choices about what children will need. In our country, we have approximately 16,000 centers of education power: 16,000 school districts, 16,000 boards of education, 16,000 superintendents of schools. And, as opposed to Russia and France, which, in effect, make one social gamble about schools, we make 16,000 different ones.

The stakes of this educational wager are high, whether we are talking about neighboring communities in this nation or competing nations. Few communities are of one mind about what future citizens will need, so that decisions about the course of the school system are frequently difficult, with several groups all wanting different kinds of programs. What finally gets taught is the result not only of the accumulation of knowledge and skills but of a political process, the struggle of a community over a classic education question: What is most worth knowing? Is it math and science? Is it how to get along with others? Is it critical thinking skills and the tools of learning? Is it character development and moral values? Or, how much of each of these priorities? Not long ago, Joseph Macekura, a junior-high principal in the state of Virginia stated:

> A school is the child of the community—fathered and mothered by all of the dreams and hopes, and bred by the frustration and hopelessness, in the hearts of its citizens . . . society's expectations of a school are ever-expanding. Like an expanding ripple in a pond created by a tossed stone, each ripple in society envelops yet another demand for the school. Where chaos exist, schools are expected to create order. Where confusion and anger exist, schools are expected to calm group and individual upheavals and substitute hope. Where individual abuse and degradation leave their indelible scars, schools are expected to regenerate, like crayfish, a new appendage of healing and stability.

In a sense, then, schools are under pressure to be all things to all people, which is another way to say that they are frequently caught amid the cross fire of a community's differing dreams and goals.

In general, though, schools tend to reflect the dominant values of their communities. In effect, we get what we pay for. But even in the best of situations, there are tensions between the school and its community. As noted, communities do not have one voice. Not only are there often competing goals, but some people, such as those with no children or with children out of school, may not be particularly interested in schools.

Another source of tension is that many people have other priorities for their tax dollars than schools, or "youth ghettoes" as they are sometimes called by nonsupporters. In the last two decades in this country, we have seen a large swing in population and social priorities from school and youth development to medical insurance and the aged. Often, those with young children and

How much of the quality of education in a community is a reflection of what the community values and supports politically?

"Aid to education sounds fine, but you and I know what will happen if the voters get too damned bright."

those who have no children in schools are in conflict over how much should be spent on children.

A third source of tension is the relationship between what the schools are currently doing and what the community wants them to do. A school-board member may give voice to a widespread concern for better writing on the part of students, but it may take several years to retrain, hire, and set in place a successful language-arts program. Until the program begins reaping tangible results and the community notices the good effects, there will be strains. Often, by the time the school has reacted positively to the community's will, there are new board members with new priorities: exit writing and enter career education or the arts.

A fourth source of tension is between particular groups in the school community. Often parents with serious academic aspirations for their children may be at odds with what they perceive as the schools' "social adjustment" emphasis or their emphasis on sports. Sometimes, working-class parents feel that the school is giving too much attention to preparation for college and too little attention to their noncollege-bound students. Often the differences become so serious that the parents move and take their children out of a public school and put them in another public school or a private school. However, this is a luxury that only the rich and the middle class can afford. The poor are stuck with the schools in their community and rarely are able to move to search for better schools.

A fifth form of tension is the tension that exists naturally between parents and those that also have a hand in raising their children. Teachers have a different function than parents. Teachers see the child in a different light, a more public light. Their focus is usually more narrow, dealing with their cognitive and social skills. They often don't see the private side of the child. They don't see the child embedded in a family network of events and aspirations. Teachers only have a slice of the child's life and lack the child's history, a history that the parents know intimately. In the early 1980's, the Boston-based columnist, Ellen Goodman, wrote about her feelings just as her daughter was graduating from the eighth grade. In her reflections, she lays bare some of the tensions that exist between the school and community members.

> The mother had brought her daughter to this school with the usual baggage of mixed emotions. She signed the girl up for learning and turned over her hours and control. Her daughter was, largely, set on her own.
>
> At times the two—parents and teachers, families and schools—formed an alliance. At times they had similar visions; at times quite the opposite. But together they made a life.
>
> From the first day to this, the last day, the mother had felt moments of uncertainty and distance from the school. On occasion she had overreacted, underreacted, misjudged events she hadn't witnessed.
>
> At times, the girl must have felt as if she were in shared custody. She uttered lines that sounded like captions for missing pictures: "But that's what the teacher told me. All the kids are doing it. You don't understand."
>
> After eight years, the mother was no longer surprised by any tension that existed between parents and schools.
>
> Even the best of schools frame another world for our children, hurt them, reward them, test them by other standards. Even the best schools separate them from us, give them other adults, other rules, other ideas. [*Boston Globe,* 8 July, 1982]

Neighboring communities in this country have different educational systems. One community will tax itself heavily for its schools. The other won't, stressing instead recreation, programs for the elderly, or letting people keep their money. One community will place a major emphasis on math and science throughout its schools; another on foreign language; yet another on physical education. At present, some communities are making a heavy investment in teaching computer literacy, while others are sticking to the "tried and true," concluding that computers are a passing fancy. Said another way, what is taught in school is a social bet, a particular community's wager concerning what its children will need to live well in the future.

The relationship between a school and its community is complicated. While everyone wants children to have a good education, there are enormous differences of opinion about what constitutes a good education. While everyone wants good schools, not everyone wants to pay for good schools. Although it may not appear so on the surface, public schools in the United States are heavily involved in the push and pull of the democratic process. Although school-board elections are rarely involved in party politics (i.e., Republican or Democrat), they are political events, where the people directly elect those candidates whose educational views they find most compatible with their own.

Thomas "Tip" O'Neil, the recently retired Speaker of the House of Representatives, once commented on national politics with the statement, "All politics is local politics." The elected public official who forgets this usually soon finds him- or herself unemployed. The same is true of school-board members and the school superintendent, the person they choose to lead the schools on a day-to-day basis. They cannot get too far away from the wishes of the community they serve. This makes the American school accountable to its citizens, who not only elect the school policy makers, the board, but also control the school's purse strings by regularly deciding how much they are willing to tax themselves in order to pay for education.

We mentioned above that American schools are distinctive in their decentralized control. These features—elected local school boards and heavy dependence on local taxing—are key in that decentralization. As opposed to countries with centralized control, with a minister of education making the decisions from the nation's capital, our schools are close to the people and accountable to them. Schools are also vulnerable to community discontent. One manifestation of this is the high turnover rate among superintendents of schools. One of the authors of this book lives in Boston, where there have been six superintendents in 11 years and recently the current superintendent's job appears in doubt.

We have emphasized the political nature of schools and the tensions that can exist in a community over schools in order to prepare you to look more critically at the school, the school system, and the community in which you are observing. To understand what goes on inside a school, it is often necessary to understand what goes on outside that school. It is important to know the community in which that school is embedded. To help you do this, we have developed and selected a number of activities and instruments.

Core Activity

Your School/Community IQ

Schools are a major part of a community. They are bound to their particular community by seen and unseen bonds, by past achievements and future hopes. Particularly in the United States, where schools are decentralized, the link between schools and community is strong. To know your school, you need to know your community. To know your community, you need to know your school.

The following exercise will enable you to test how much you know about a particular community and its schools. Do this exercise either in your home community and its schools or in the school and community in which you are currently observing. If you are in doubt about which to do, check with your instructor.

This test will confront you with issues you may never have considered or for which you do not have answers. Where you do not have a ready answer, try to think it through. Where you do not have exact information, make an educated guess.

Student Name _____   Date _____

The Community

(1) If an interested friend asked you to describe this community, what are some of the things you would tell him or her? Try to be as detailed as possible in your answer.

_____

_____

_____

_____

_____

_____

_____

_____

(2) What is the population (approximately) of people in your community?

_____

(3) How large is your community? _____ miles wide; _____ miles long.

(4) What are the major sources of income of the people in your community?

a.

b.

c.

d.

e.

f.

(5) Estimate the percentage of the working population in each of the following occupational groups.

_____% Type 1—Small business owner
_____% Type 2—Skilled worker (secretary, nurse's aide, technician, etc.)
_____% Type 3—Professional (doctor, lawyer, architect)
_____% Type 4—Public servant (politician, government worker)
_____% Type 5—Teacher or in education
_____% Type 6—Laborer (factory worker)
_____% Type 7—Tradesperson (plumber, carpenter, machinist)
_____% Type 8—Business executive, management, salesperson
_____% Type 9—Farmer
_____% Type 10—Homemaker
_____% Type 11—Other (specify) _____

(6) What percentage of the adult women work outside of the home? _____

(7) What is your estimate of the major religious groups in your community?

_____% Protestant

_____% Catholic

_____% Jewish

_____% Other (specify) _____

(8) List the percentage of each of these groups in your community.

_____% White Americans

_____% Black Americans

_____% Asian-Americans

_____% Hispanic-American

_____% Other (specify)

(9) List and estimate the percentage of the major ethnic and/or national groups in your community.

_____% _____

_____% _____

_____% _____

_____% _____

Student Name _____   Date _____

(10) How would you describe the current state of your community? As a vital, growing community? As an old, but still vital, community? As a slowly decaying community? Describe in your own words what you believe to be the health of your community.

_____

_____

_____

_____

_____

_____

_____

_____

(11) What percentage of your community are "newcomers"? _____% Do

people in this community refer to "newcomers" as "outsiders"? _____

What percentage of the people currently residing in the community

would you estimate have gone to the local schools? _____%

(12) In your judgment, is your community a good place for young people to grow up? Why or why not?

_____

_____

_____

_____

_____

_____

_____

(13) Thinking broadly about the education in your community, list the educational institutions where learning goes on. Do not just confine yourself to the public and private schools.

a.

b.

c.

d.

e.

f.

g.

h.

i.

j.

k.

l.

m.

n.

o.

p.

q.

r.

s.

Is there competition among any of these institutions? If so, how would you describe it?

The School

1. In general, do you believe that teachers in your community are respected? Why or why not?

2. Where do the teachers reside in the community?

   ____% Live in the community

   ____% Live outside the community

3. What percentage of teachers went to the local elementary and secondary schools when they were young? _____%

4. On the average, do teachers make as much money as the majority of people in the community? _____

5. How would you describe the relationship between the teachers that you know well and the people in the community?

6. What evidence do you see of teachers drawing on the resources, both personal and institutional, from the community?

7. Summarize your views on the relationships among the school, the teachers, and the community.

8. How would you describe our own attitudes toward this community? Is it a place where you would like to teach? Is it a place where you would like to live?

NOTE: If you had trouble filling out this School/Community questionnaire, you may wish to get some help. The city or town hall is often a good source of general information about a community. So, too, are the local newspapers and the chamber of commerce. Because it is important for school administrators to know their community, they often have much of the kind of information requested here at their fingertips. Finally, the teachers and administrators in the school in which you are observing may be another source of information and insight to help you answer these questions.

Student Name _____   Date _____

Suggested Activity One
Community Member Interview

In this next activity, get the views of three community members (ideally, one should be a school-board member) on the following questions.

1. How would you describe the community's support for its schools?
   Community member 1:

   Community member 2:

   Community member 3:

2. How would you describe the community's willingness to pay for good schools?
   Community member 1:

Community member 2:

Community member 3:

3. What aspects of a school tend to be most heavily supported, or what is most favorably viewed by the community?
Community member 1:

Community member 2:

Community member 3:

4. What are the strongest criticisms that are heard about the schools from community members?
   Community member 1:

   Community member 2:

   Community member 3:

Student Name _____   Date _____

Suggested Activity Two
Educator Interview

Pick three different educators (ideally an experienced teacher, a new teacher, and an administrator) from the school in which you are observing and ask them each of the following questions.

1. How would you describe the community's support for their schools?
   Educator 1:

   Educator 2:

   Educator 3:

2. How would you describe the community's willingness to pay for good schools?

Educator 1:

Educator 2:

Educator 3:

3. What aspects of a school tend to be most heavily supported, or what is most favorably viewed by the community?

Educator 1:

Educator 2:

Educator 3:

4. What are the strongest criticisms that are heard about the schools from community members?
Educator 1:

Educator 2:

Educator 3:

Student Name _____   Date _____

Suggested Activity Three
Truth or Exaggeration

When social conditions change, schools change. What a community expects of its school, or demands of its school, shifts with new social priorities. Ten years ago a group of educators in Ohio wrote the mock job-opening announcement below. The description tells a lot about the realities of teaching, but also exaggerates a great deal.

As you read through "Personnel Wanted" underline what you feel are exaggerations and put checkmarks next to the more realistic points.

PERSONNEL WANTED

Openings are available in a variety of areas for special people. Are you in a rut? No variety in your present position? Are you a professional-type person who loves children and a challenge? Check the following requirements and see if you qualify.

QUALIFICATIONS

At least a bachelor's degree (with an average of two additional years of college work).

You Should Also Be . . .

loving . . . arts/craftsy . . . athletic . . . resourceful . . . understanding . . . creative . . . loyal . . . enthusiastic . . . organized . . . dependable . . . knowledgeable . . . responsible to leadership . . . aware of fads . . . committed . . . able to update antiquated materials . . . accountable . . . fair disciplinarian . . . unfailingly cheerful . . . well-read . . . respectful . . . alert . . . quick decision maker . . . willing volunteer . . . multitalented . . . wise . . . charismatic . . . psychic . . . trivia expert . . . mechanically inclined . . . able to please everyone all of the time . . . honest . . . strong in nerves . . . sensitive . . . tactful . . . mentally and physically healthy . . . diplomatic . . . fair . . . diverse interests . . . well informed . . . patient . . . attractive . . . unflappable . . . superhuman in stamina . . . not easily frustrated . . . able to enunciate . . . physically strong . . . community oriented . . . able to function in crisis situations . . . ABLE TO TEACH!

FURTHER REQUIREMENTS

You Must Be Able to . . .

keep records . . . collect money . . . coach . . . support school functions (monetarily) . . . plan a curriculum . . . write behavioral objectives . . . write lesson plans . . . write reports of all kinds . . . attend seminars, athletic events, plays, carnivals, festivals, musicals, fund-raising events, parent–teacher organization meetings, graduations, committee meetings, school-board meetings, department meetings, faculty meetings.

And Be Able to . . .

supervise lunchroom, recess, halls, bathrooms, study hall, detention, assemblies, plays, student council . . . prepare infallible testing instruments, create the perfect testing environment . . . evaluate all work . . . provide guidance . . . break up fights . . . check students for drugs and/or alcohol . . . deal with discipline . . . maintain a quiet classroom . . . interpret medical records.

Must Be a(n) . . .

secretary . . . advisor . . . photographer . . . ticket-taker . . . librarian . . . curriculum developer . . . veterinarian . . . plumber . . . mechanic . . . biologist . . . handwriting expert . . . typist . . . interior decorator . . . entertainer . . . lecturer . . . janitor . . . carpenter . . . electrician . . . diagnostician . . . chauffeur . . . chaperone . . . nurse . . . statistician . . . dishwasher . . . housekeeper . . . psychiatrist . . . confidant . . . leader . . . cook . . . host/hostess . . . mathematician . . . historian . . . nutritionist . . . politician . . . accountant . . . linguist . . . cryptologist . . . author . . . companion . . . friend . . . file clerk . . . office machines expert . . . tear dryer . . . hand holder . . . back patter . . . shoulder lender . . . ego builder . . . shoe tier . . . nose wiper . . . boot tugger . . . clothes zipper . . . lost-book finder . . . problem solver . . . father/mother confessor . . . advisor to the lovelorn.

WORKING CONDITIONS

- One book, chair, and desk you may have to share (the desk doesn't lock)
- Poor lighting, heating, and circulation
- Inadequate restroom and medical facilities
- Infrequent or nonexistent breaks with the exception of ½ hour for lunch and calls of a personal nature
- Institutional food (if you have the time and/or appetite)

FRINGE BENEFITS

- All the gum you can scrape off the bottoms of desks
- A growing collection of broken pencils, confiscated squirt guns, and miscellaneous animals, insects, and reptiles
- Vocabulary development (you will learn many new words)
- Exposure to original graffiti and love letters
- More free advice than you can use
- Opportunity to move from assignment to assignment; from class to class; from school to school
- High esteem in your community
- Exposure to various pathogens

If you feel you have the qualifications, if you love a challenge, contact your local school-board office for an application.

Student Name _____   Date _____

Journal Entry

Your observation and study of your current school should focus on the relations between the school and the community it is serving and by which it is being supported. In this journal entry, consider the following questions and issues:

1. What tensions exist between the school and the community?

2. To what degree are the teachers "of the community"? Are they similar, socially and educationally, to the majority of the parents whose children they teach? Do they live there? Do they reflect the values of the community?

3. What aspects of the school program (sports, dramatics, vocational programs, foreign-language programs) receive a good deal of support from the community?

4. What is the evidence that the community financially supports the school? What is the physical condition of the school? Does the school have an adequate gym? Auditorium? Library? Computer labs? How does the teachers' salary compare to teachers' salaries in neighboring communities?

_____

_____

_____

_____

_____

_____

_____

_____

_____

_____

_____

Questions for Discussion

1. If schools were to disappear, along with the idea of schooling, what are some other ways we might invent to prepare the young for adulthood?

2. How would the life of your family be changed if its members were responsible for the bulk of your education? What would be gained and what would be lost?

3. Selecting either the school/community in which you are currently observing or your "home" school/community (the one you know best), discuss the major tensions that exist between the school and the community.

4. What are some things teachers, administrators, and students can do to strengthen the bonds between students and their communities?

Interpreting Metaphors of Schooling

For the most part, you've been observing and analyzing classroom activities and interviewing and interpreting the feelings of classroom teachers. You've also been asked to evaluate whether the school you're observing in represents an effective school based on some specific criteria. In the process of performing these activities, you may have noticed yourself reflecting upon your school experiences and trying to project your feelings about school into the setting you were observing. This is a natural inclination of observers; most observers attempt to understand a present reality by projecting it upon a screen of previously established realities. Sometimes we help ourselves in this process through the use of *metaphors*.

Every school environment contains subtle, implicit, or hidden realities that carry powerful messages to those who are immersed in the environment. These realities and the lessons they silently teach are sometimes referred to as the "hidden" curriculum. What is particularly interesting about the hidden curriculum is that we often recall elements contained in it for much longer than we recall the subjects we studied in the explicit curriculum. For example, you may have long ago forgotten the words you spelled correctly or misspelled in your school's spelling contests, but you will probably never forget the feeling of consistently winning or regularly going out early in the match. In the area of math, you may need considerable prompting to remember how to work out a quadratic equation, yet you can easily conjure up the image of your math teacher demanding that you get to class on time and the punishments meted out when that rule was broken. Finally, you may not recall specific lunches you ate during high school, but the cafeteria ambience is easily remembered.

These elements of competition, compliance, and atmosphere create impressions of school that span both time and space. For many individuals, the hidden curriculum established common images for depicting the school experience. The common images are so vivid that we can easily express them by way of metaphors. Some individuals, when asked to describe their schools, respond that it was "like a prison," or "a zoo." Others describe it as similar to being in a "factory" or "like living in a little community." What each of these responses is doing, metaphorically, is capturing and synthesizing several hidden curricular elements of the school and then projecting them by way of the metaphor. Interestingly, the metaphors, along with our own memories and common images of school experience establish a bond that eliminates a considerable amount of extensive, behavioral descriptions. We'll look at some examples of these metaphors later in the chapter.

While these metaphorical attempts to understand and compress the complexities of the school environment can be extremely useful in your initial observations, you must recognize the effect they have on your thinking. By projecting the environment you're trying to understand upon either your past experiences or a familiar metaphor, you may be inclined to distort the environment so that it no longer represents what you're actually observing.

For example, during initial observations, a student might discover that his or her cooperating teacher utilizes classroom-management strategies similar to those employed by one of the student's former teachers. Because of this, the student may be inclined to look for other similarities in an attempt to relate the unfamiliar behaviors of the cooperating teacher to the familiar behaviors of the former teacher. Ultimately, the student's portrayal of that classroom's environment reflects more of what the student wants to see rather than what he or she is actually seeing.

This phenomenon can occur among observers of diverse cultures as well when in an effort to understand tribal mores and folkways, the observer focuses too heavily on marital customs, for example, instead of courtship customs because his or her own cultural experiences did not emphasize elaborate courtship rituals. Rather than an accurate, unique portrayal of village (or classroom) life, one gets a picture that has been focused and narrowed through the experiential lens of the observer. As a result, the observations, field notes, and journal entries tend to reveal more about the observer's biases than what new information the observer has discovered about a specific cultures based upon his or her observations of that unique environment.

Although the use of metaphor can be less distorting than the lens of prior experience, it still has the potential to be misleading. This occurs when we allow the metaphor to create the structure of reality we are perceiving rather than creating a metaphor to fit the reality we are trying to understand. The relationship between reality and the metaphor we use to depict it is critical. The metaphor is a lens through which we look at reality; it is not a reality itself. The metaphor creates a lens through which reality is viewed, at times exaggerating some features and suppressing others (Kliebard, 1985). It must be clearly understood, however, that the metaphor is allowing us to organize our thinking, in this case, about schools and schooling.

A common metaphor used in describing schools is that of a factory (Grannis, 1967). The students are raw materials and ultimately products, the teachers are workers, the principal is a foreman, supervisor, or general manager, the superintendent is the company president and the school board is the board of directors. The curriculum, of course, is part of the machinery or technology that molds and shapes the raw material into the product desired. Extending the metaphor further, one could compare competency testing and accountability to quality control and product warranties. Even the hours schools are open are analogous to those of the day shift in a factory and some schools have time clocks where teachers "punch in."

The paradox of this metaphor is that it is both conceptually rich and philosophically misleading. If the metaphor is taken too literally, we begin to observe only those phenomena that reinforce the factory metaphor. We look for examples of situations where students are being molded, manipulated, and controlled so that they all come out the same (product integrity). We look for teachers who are acting as though they are workers routinely performing mechanical tasks. We look for administrators whose sole purpose seems to be keeping the "workers" "on task," and teachers who do likewise.

The danger here, of course, is that we lose the richness of the situation because our metaphorical lens prevents us from seeing or thinking about nonfactory elements of schools. We fail to recognize other metaphors that could be equally revealing, for example, the school as a garden, the school as a family, the school as a community, and so on. This does not negate the usefulness of the factory metaphor; it only suggests that other metaphors may be used in conjunction with the factory metaphor to create an even richer vision and understanding of the classroom and school. In these examples, the factory, the garden, the community, and so on, are the metaphors and the classrooms or schools are the reality.

As you observe in classrooms, your attempts to objectively record activities, behaviors, expressions of feelings, and so on, may sound more subjective than objective upon later reading. Both your prior experience in schools and the natural tendency to describe situations metaphorically contribute to this subjectivity. While these dual lenses might seem to be distorting reality, they can also serve a useful purpose if used cautiously.

Recent work in the field of education has indicated that we need to broaden the way we observe and evaluate classrooms and schools (Eisner, 1979). Much of this literature suggests that while objective or quantifiable observation devices yield important data, these data cannot fully reveal the contextual richness of the situation being observed. Researchers believe that observers must be sensitive to certain *qualities* that exist in classrooms and schools or among teachers, and that these qualities need to be identified and discussed. Not surprisingly, this type of observation has been called *qualitative* research.

You've already been identifying quantifiable phenomena in earlier chapters, and you've also been doing some qualitative analyses on an intuitive basis in your journal entries. Our purpose now is to introduce activities that will prepare you to perform these qualitative observations more effectively. To do this you will need to employ your dual lenses of prior experience and metaphorical thinking carefully and flexibly. If you do this, your dual lenses, like a binocular, will allow you to focus in clearly on the complex reality of class-rooms and schools.

For the most part, your prior observations asked you to record specific behaviors, activities, elements, and so on, as you saw them occurring or existing in the school or classroom. You were then asked to draw some conclusions based upon these objective data. At that point, you were expected to "call them as you saw them" and not to infer more than the data revealed. Now, by way of example, we'll see how that form of information gathering might be enriched qualitatively.

As part of your observations you may have recorded incidences where teachers used *desist* behaviors. These behaviors involved such teacher strategies as moving closer to students who were inattentive or talking, placing a hand on an inattentive student's shoulder while continuing to lecture, placing an index finger vertically by the mouth to signal the need for quiet, and switching the lights off to gain student attention at the beginning of a lesson or during a transitional activity. On the basis of simply recording these strategies as desist behaviors, one might conclude that each was equally effective or appropriate because each one "worked" (i.e., attained the desired result). This is clearly a premature judgment.

On the one hand, the observer has objectively captured the teacher's behaviors and categorized them correctly. On the other hand, however, the observer has leaped to the conclusion that each desist behavior is equally effective. This is a tendency among beginning teacher observers. Because they are anxious to identify strategies that "work" so they can add them to their repertoire of emerging teacher behaviors, they, and possibly you, tend not to discriminate among these behaviors to determine if they are truly as effective as they appear to be. This tends to occur most often with classroom-management behaviors.

From a qualitative perspective, you should begin to analyze the context in which a desist behavior occurs. This can be done by responding to the questions in suggested activity one. While not exhaustive, the list of questions will begin to get you thinking about the qualitative dimension surrounding your objective observation. You will use your prior experiences, values, and perhaps some metaphors to describe your reaction to these behaviors.

Another example will illustrate how you might express the qualitative aspects of your objective observational data metaphorically. As you recall from Chapter Four, you were asked to record what appeared to be on-task and off-task student behaviors and to assess the amount of engaged time for selected students in the classroom. Quantitatively, you were in a position to draw some inferences about the effective use of time in certain classrooms, grade levels, and content areas.

Although these inferences enabled you to see observable aspects of the classroom more efficiently, you may have felt the need to elaborate more extensively on the meaning of time, the juxtaposition of work (on-task) and play (off-task) behaviors, and the necessity for maintaining a businesslike atmosphere in schools. These feelings might best be explored qualitatively and metaphorically as you complete Suggested Activity Two.

The purpose for expanding your observations qualitatively is to stretch your imagination, thus enabling you to examine and describe classrooms from multiple perspectives. Ultimately, you may find yourself in conflict with several of your metaphorical sketches and qualitative descriptions, but that's the nature of multiple perspectives. The result will be a greatly expanded set of tools for reflecting on your own classroom behaviors as well as the behaviors of others. This will develop your skills as a critical (i.e., discriminating) observer of schools and enhance your ability to explain why a particular teaching or classroom-management strategy not only works for a given set of students but is also philosophically appropriate for that classroom and school.

What metaphor could you create that would describe what this cartoonist is trying to convey about schools?

"Sorry kids, but this is the newest map we could afford."

originally published in Phi Delta Kappan

Student Name _____   Date _____

Core Activity

In the activity below, you will complete the chart that contains several common metaphors for schools. In the additional space, create your own metaphor(s) for schools and expand upon it as you did in the other examples. A blank chart is included on the next page for you to use with your cooperating teacher(s).

Common Metaphors

School as:	Teacher as:	Child as:	Curriculum as:
1. Factory	Worker	Raw Material	Machinery/Tools
2. Minisociety	Bureaucrat	Citizen	Laws of Conduct
3. Football Game	Coach	Player	Game Plan
4. Prison			
5. Garden			
6. Zoo			
7. Child-Care Center			
8. Spaceship			
9. Xerox Machine			
10.			

Student Name _____   Date _____

Core Activity (Cooperating Teacher)

Common Metaphors

School as:	Teacher as:	Child as:	Curriculum as:
1. Factory	Worker	Raw Material	Machinery/Tools
2. Minisociety	Bureaucrat	Citizen	Laws of Conduct
3. Football Game	Coach	Player	Game Plan
4. Prison			
5. Garden			
6. Zoo			
7. Child-Care Center			
8. Spaceship			
9. Xerox Machine			
10.			

Suggested Activity One
Interpreting Desist Behaviors

1. Was a desist behavior really necessary? Why?

2. What immediately preceded and followed the desist behavior?

3. How did the student(s) react to the desist behavior?

4. How did the teacher employ the desist behavior (i.e., was it natural or contrived)?

5. Could *you* employ the desist behavior(s) effectively? Under what conditions?

6. Was there something about the desist behavior that bothered you? What was it, and why did it bother you?

Suggested Activity Two

Interpreting On-Task/Off-Task Behaviors

---

1. Discuss the hidden curricular aspects of on-task behaviors of students. What is this type of regimen analogous to? What do students learn from this?

2. How do you think students perceive work and play in school? Which has the dominant role and how do the activities of work and play interact in the course of a school day? Compare similar concepts as you did with work and play (e.g., industriousness vs. idleness, Protestant ethic vs. hedonism, control vs. autonomy).

3. How does compliance with rules of the school prepare one for fulfilling roles in business and industry as an adult?

Suggested Activity Three

The Hidden Curriculum

As indicated earlier in the chapter, the hidden curriculum sends powerful messages to students through a variety of channels. These messages are usually presented unconsciously and are not part of the planned curriculum. In your observations of the school and classroom, you should begin identifying the context within which these messages are sent. In the space following, provide examples of ways in which the messages listed were transmitted to students.

1. "The classroom or school is a competitive and highly individualistic learning environment."

_____

_____

_____

_____

2. "Students who comply with rules and norms will get into less trouble than those who don't."

_____

_____

_____

_____

3. "There is always some way to beat the system."

_____

_____

_____

_____

4. "There is a certain 'classroom etiquette' that differs from classroom to classroom."

_____

_____

_____

_____

5. "Work is more important than play."

_____

_____

_____

_____

6. "Schools and classrooms resemble 'class' societies (i.e., have lower-, middle-, and upper-class structures operating)."

_____

_____

_____

_____

7. "The well-being of the group is more important than individual autonomy."

_____

_____

_____

_____

Student Name _____   Date _____

Journal Entry

This chapter concentrated on observing the total environment of the classroom and school by expanding upon the quantitative data gathering you did in earlier chapters. Your journal entry should reflect a more *qualitative* approach to recording your thoughts and feelings. In this entry, you should experiment with metaphorical descriptions and analogies that demonstrate your insights into the total school environment, especially the hidden curriculum. Try your hand at the following:

1. Express your feelings about the positive and negative effects of the hidden curriculum in the classroom or school you're observing. How do you feel about the "lessons" students are receiving in competition, compliance, etiquette, and so on?

2. Capture the entire landscape of the classroom you're in through a metaphor (or analogy). Where does your analogy work and where does it break down? Can you create another metaphor that more adequately captures or summarizes the classroom reality you're observing?

3. Identify to what extent your perceptions of this classroom are affected by your previous experiences in school. Did any of your observations trigger a recollection of a particular teacher or class that you had?

4. Describe ways in which your understanding of schools is expanding when you view schools from a teacher's, a student's, and an outside observer's perspective.

Student Name _____   Date _____

_____

_____

_____

_____

_____

_____

_____

_____

_____

_____

_____

_____

_____

_____

_____

_____

_____

_____

_____

_____

_____

_____

_____

_____

_____

_____

_____

_____

_____

_____

Questions for Discussion

1. What are some of the hidden messages that teachers and schools send to students and how do students modify their behaviors based on these messages? In what ways do students resist these modifications?

2. Describe some of the enduring lessons you learned from your school experiences that may not have been part of the planned curriculum. Discuss how those experiences helped develop you into the kind of learner you are now. How might that affect the way you teach?

3. Select a teacher behavior that you felt worked well given the teacher's objective (e.g., introducing a topic in an interesting and attention-grabbing manner). Analyze that strategy to determine why it worked both from the students' and teacher's point of view. Is it a strategy you could perform equally well? In what ways would it be less effective for you and how could you improve upon it?

4. How do metaphors or analogies enrich observations of classrooms and schools? How can they distort the realities they're supposed to be clarifying? Describe ways to reduce this distortion.

References

Chiarelott, L., T. Onder, and C. M. Nicoloff. (1988). Metaphorical thinking: Implications for curriculum and teaching. Paper presented at the Bergamo Curriculum Theory Conf. Dayton, Oh., Oct., 1988.

Eisner, E. (1979). *The educational imagination.* New York: Macmillan.

Grannis J. (Fall, 1967). The school as a model of society. *Harvard Graduate School of Education Bulletin,* 21, 25–27.

Kliebard, H. M. (1985). Curriculum theory as metaphor. *Theory into Practice,* 21 (1), 112–17.

Lawton, D. (1984). Metaphor and the Curriculum. In *Metaphors of Education,* edited by Wm. Taylor. London: Heineman Educational Books, 79–80.

Pratte, R. (1981). Metaphorical models and curriculum theory. *Curriculum Inquiry,* 307–320.

Quina, J. (1989). *Effective secondary teaching.* New York: Harper & Row, 222–248.

Samples, B. (1976). *The metaphoric mind.* Reading, Mass: Addison-Wesley.

CHAPTER 9

Embracing the Challenge of Diversity and Individual Differences in American Classrooms

At this point in American history, when you consider teaching as a possible career, you should realize, first, that you are making a positive statement about yourself vis-à-vis diversity, and, second, that it is a highly appropriate time to make such a statement. Today, in many parts of the United States, classrooms are becoming even more diverse as immigrants and refugees from various parts of the world find their way into the United States.

The teaching profession, in all 50 states, in more than 1,200 teacher-training institutions, and in approximately 16,000 school districts, has accepted, at varying levels of intensity, the responsibility and challenge of educating highly diverse groups of students to their fullest potential. This commitment to support diversity, which implies a pervasive and consistent attention to individual differences, is a part of the tradition, symbolic rhetoric, and legislative framework of American education; it is what makes the American classroom unique among the classrooms of the world. In contemporary American classrooms, the diversity in the student body's language background, culture and ethnicity, religious background, learning aptitude, achievement rate, family structure, stability, socioeconomic status, and learning problems makes teaching a particularly fascinating and potentially rewarding career.

Potentially is a useful word to focus on here. Classroom diversity can prove to be challenging, exciting, and satisfying, but it can also be frightening, frustrating, and overwhelming. While your teacher-education program will likely provide you with skills and knowledge to meet the challenge of diversity, your own personality and comfort level will also be a factor in determining how classroom diversity will affect your teaching and career. With this perspective in mind, our activities will introduce you to positive examples of teachers who have successfully embraced the challenge of diversity. This will make your choice to become or not become a teacher more informed and reality-based. Let us turn now to some terms and definitions that are connected to this discussion.

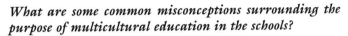

What are some common misconceptions surrounding the purpose of multicultural education in the schools?

"Of course it's misspelled. I'm preserving my indigenous cultural dialect."

The diversity and attention to individual differences alluded to above stem from several sources in American culture and history, and is discussed in the popular literature, as well as college courses, under various headings. Some of the more common are: multicultural education; special education; bilingual/bicultural education; individualized instruction; and learning styles. Some brief remarks about these terms will help to introduce the core activity and suggested activities for this chapter.

In the group of terms above, *multicultural education* has the broadest sweep. Most educational writers perceive multicultural education as a political movement or reform process within education and the larger culture; a decisive point in this movement is widely assumed to be the Supreme Court's desegregation decision in *Brown* v. *the Board of Education* in 1954. The major goal of the movement has been to create schools in which a wide range of cultural groups, such as women and disabled persons, and ethnic groups, such as Black Americans and Hispanic Americans will experience educational equity. Educational equity here implies the opportunity to study in schools that are equally funded, and dedicated to creating optimal academic success for all students. The classroom instruction that derives from the goal of equity is aimed at the development of citizens who are prepared—in terms of knowledge, attitudes, and skills—to build, and productively participate in, an integrated, pluralistic, equal-opportunity-oriented, democratic society. In simplest terms, multicultural education, at the classroom level, leads to a special and vigorous form of citizenship education.

The same could not be said for *special education*, a term that also describes a movement; however, this movement has a narrower focus. Special education is, as noted, part of the multicultural reform process, but also independent of it in the minds and hearts of many educators. In public school settings special educators have special training and licenses, and are responsible for establishing fair and optimal learning environments for students who have learning disabilities or more serious educational handicaps. Mainstreaming, an educational strategy that attempts to provide the least restrictive (or most optimal) learning environment for such students, increasingly brings large numbers of special-education students into regular education classrooms, which is referred to as the mainstream of the school setting. When this occurs, a special educator will discuss with a regular educator, the individual education plan (IEP) that has been drawn up by the special educator, parents, and other school site or district educators. Increasingly, these mandatory IEPs attempt to take into account the student's learning style or preferences as they identify specific goals and suggested learning activities for the student in question. As used here, learning style means, and consists of, those variables that describe the way the individual prefers to, or best learns, new and difficult information. For example, in a dialogue, parents, student, special educator, and the regular classroom teacher might decide that a particular child would benefit from having a portable tape recorder available for his or her use throughout the day.

Bilingual education, English as a second language (ESL), limited English proficient (LEP) and other terms point to another aspect of diversity in our nation. The current wave of immigration into the United States is bringing hundreds of thousands of ESL/LEP, or bilingual learners, into the classes you will teach. These children are coming into American schools that no longer try to melt away all their cultural and language differences. Today, the appreciation, indeed the celebration and utilization of these differences, along with a strong emphasis on English literacy, is part and parcel of the complex equation of multicultural education, an equation to which you will contribute in one way or another.

It should be clear from the above that one of the greatest joys and challenges you will experience as a teacher will stem from your attempt to sensitively and wisely respond to the diversity of sociocultural backgrounds and instructional needs your students will bring to your classroom. Your ability to respond positively and appropriately to this challenge will be strongly influenced by the knowledge and skills you possess vis-à-vis responding to diversity, and your own attitudes regarding diversity. Traditionally, when considering a career in teaching, prospective teachers—particularly those oriented toward elementary teaching—have been asked to consider whether or not they really like children. An equally valid question for today's prospective teacher is: As a teacher, would you welcome and value diversity in your classroom? Certainly as stated, this broad question is not easy to answer, but you can gain some insight into your feelings about classroom diversity by completing the core activity, as well as other selected activities listed below. Please note that the Core Activity specifies a certain type of classroom for observation. In some areas of the United States, such an integrated classroom will be difficult to locate for every student in the program. Our desire is to have prospective teachers observe teachers who respond to diversity in an exemplary manner. The degree of specific ethnic diversity is less important that the expertise manifested by the teacher. We appreciate also that some teacher-education programs operate almost totally in environments that are rich in diversity. In such areas, the activities in this chapter may be redundant, or they may reinforce and extend what is the normal pattern of prestudent-teaching observation.

Core Activity
Observing Diversity in the Classroom

Observe for a full day or two half days in an upper (fourth, fifth, or sixth grade, junior-high or high-school) classroom that has a rich diversity of ethnic and racial groups represented (approximately 50 percent nonwhite, if possible), as well as several students who are limited English proficient, or students who have learning disabilities of one kind or another. The teacher you observe should be identified as a successful teacher by your professor, and if possible, the classroom should be in a school considered to be lower S.E.S. (socioeconomic status) in the school district. After your observation, do the following:

1. Answer these questions:
   (a) How would you feel if you were assigned to teach as a student teacher (or teacher) in this classroom? Would you want to teach in this classroom? In this school? Why or why not?

2. Conduct an informal, semistructured interview with the teacher and/or the principal of the school. Try to discuss how the teacher and/or principal:
   (a) thinks and feels about the classroom diversity he or she encounters; and
   (b) defines multicultural education and multicultural instruction.

Write a few paragraphs that compare and contrast your interviewee's perceptions of classroom diversity and multicultural education with those presented in this chapter. Where possible, share your findings with other prospective teachers.

Suggested Activity One
Observing Multicultural Settings

Observe for a full day or two half days in a classroom that mirrors the following characteristics as closely as possible:

1. Predominantly middle-class white students (60–90%);
2. Ten to forty percent visible ethnic students (Black American or Hispanic, American or Native-American, or Asian-American);
3. Several students who are mainstreamed;
4. The school you observe in should be considered a middle-class school by the school's principal.

After the day's observation complete the following activities:

1. Answer these questions:
   (a) Did the teaching, learning, and classroom interaction in this classroom differ from that of the classroom you observed in your core activity? Did it differ from other classrooms you have observed in?
   (b) How would you feel if you were assigned to teach as a student teacher or first-year teacher in this classroom? Would you want to teach in this classroom? School? Why? Why not?
2. Conduct an informal, semistructured interview with the teacher and/or the principal of the school. Try to discover how the teacher and/or principal:
   (a) feels about the level of classroom or school diversity he or she works with;
   (b) handles policies associated with mainstreaming;
   (c) orients teaching and evaluation toward a better match with students' special learning styles; and
   (d) views and defines multicultural education.

Write a few paragraphs that compare and contrast your interviewee's perceptions of multicultural education with those presented in this chapter. Does your interviewee make a connection between multicultural education and special education (the education that mainstreamed and other exceptional children receive)? Where possible, share your findings with other prospective teachers.

Suggested Activity Two
Observing the Special Needs Classroom

Most elementary, junior high, and high schools have special rooms and special teachers who work individually or in small groups with students who require special instruction for one reason or another. The teachers who provide this instruction will typically have received extensive training to prepare them for this special role, which includes providing support for the regular classroom teachers in the school. For the purpose of learning how to deal with diversity in the classroom, these resource-room or special educators can be a valuable resource for prospective teachers. To tap into this resource complete the following.

1. Observe in a resource room for an entire morning, making special note of the physical differences between the resource classroom and the regular classroom. In the way of resources, what does the resource room have that the regular classroom doesn't? In addition, observe and take notes on the way the resource-room teacher interacts with his or her students. Please note that in your region or state, the resource room may have a different name. Seek out the room where individualized instruction for mainstreamed students with special learning needs is provided.

2. Conduct an informal, semistructured interview with the resource-room teacher. Try to discover:

   (a) if the resource-room teacher makes use of learning-style data or any other type of special information in designing effective instruction for his or her students.

   (b) what the resource-room teacher believes the regular classroom teacher can do in his or her own classroom to create supportive, enabling learning environments for diverse learners.

   (c) if the resource-room teacher believes there are specific teaching strategies or approaches to teaching that would benefit most of the children he or she teaches.

3. Write a few paragraphs that summarize what you have learned about creating supportive, enabling learning environments for students with special learning needs. Where possible, share your findings with other prospective teachers.

Suggested Activity Three
Observing Learning/Teaching Styles

It is widely assumed that teachers who are adept at creating supportive, enabling learning environments for diverse students are able to do so because they have developed a flexible teaching style. They have developed an ability and commitment to flex toward the diverse learning style and needs of their students. Sometimes, this ability and proclivity to flex begins with a heightened awareness of their own learning style and needs. Completion of the worksheet below, followed up by class or small-group discussions, should prove to be an illuminating exercise.

The learning- and teaching-style-analysis worksheet has been used in a variety of teacher-education courses (Davidman, 1984). The worksheet is filled out after several different conceptions of learning style are discussed. The learning-style conceptions of Joseph Renzulli, Linda Smith, Rita Dunn, and Gary Price, while different, have served as useful stimuli for teachers' self-analysis of their own learning style. Renzulli and Smith define learning style in terms of the teaching strategies students prefer to learn by. The strategies presented in their instrument are:

1. Projects
2. Drill and Recitation
3. Peer Teaching
4. Discussion
5. Teaching Games
6. Independent Study
7. Programmed Instruction
8. Lecture
9. Simulation

The Dunn/Price conception and instrument, on the other hand, incorporates a wide range of variables that affect the way learners concentrate on, absorb, and retain new or difficult information and skills. The variables, which are listed below, are environmental, sociological, physical, and psychological in nature. The wide-ranging Dunn/Price conception is valuable because it reminds us that for some learners an environmental variable like light or warmth may be as critical to learning success as a teaching strategy. The Dunn/Price variables are:

Prefers learning several ways

Auditory preferences

Visual preferences

Tactile preferences

Kinesthetic preferences

Requires intake

Functions best in morning

Functions best in late morning

Functions best in afternoon

Functions best in evening

Needs mobility

Sound

Light

Warmth

Formal design

Motivated/unmotivated

Adult-motivated

Teacher-motivated

Persistent

Responsible

Structure

Prefers learning alone

Peer-oriented learner

Learning with adults

Instructions

Before you begin filling in the following worksheet, try to identify some of the best and worst learning experiences you've had in the past five or so years. Then as you complete these sentences use these learning experiences as a source of data. In addition, for 1 through 3, think about school *and* home learning environments, paying particular attention to the teachers' strategies, structure of the class, and any cognitive, affective, or environmental variables that you consider pertinent. Use the back of the page if you need more room, and please refer to the Dunn/Price and Renzulli/Smith lists above as you complete this form. Answer 7 and 8 only if you have had teaching experience.

Student Name _____   Date _____

Worksheet

1. I learn new and/or difficult information best when:

    (a) _____

    (b) _____

    (c) _____

    (d) _____

    (e) _____

    (f) _____

    (g) _____

2. I have trouble learning new and/or difficult information when:

    (a) _____

    (b) _____

    (c) _____

    (d) _____

    (e) _____

    (f) _____

    (g) _____

3. I find it *very* helpful to my learning if the learning environment is, or has:

    (a) _____

    (b) _____

    (c) _____

    (d) _____

    (e) _____

    (f) _____

    (g) _____

Student Name _____   Date _____

4. When I study, whether at home or school, I like to:

  (a) _____

  (b) _____

  (c) _____

  (d) _____

  (e) _____

  (f) _____

5. The way I learn is probably like that of others in many ways, but I think it may be special because I:

  (a) _____

  (b) _____

  (c) _____

6. Between elementary school and today, my learning style preferences/ needs have:

  ☐ remained pretty much the same

  ☐ changed moderately (please describe the change(s) below)

  ☐ have changed a great deal (please describe the change(s) below)

_____

_____

_____

_____

_____

_____

_____

Student Name _____   Date _____

7. Regarding my teaching style, in my teaching I will likely make good use of the following teaching strategies (or would if the resources were available). Put an X in the boxes in front of the appropriate strategies, and please fill in your own strategies if they are not here.

☐ Discuss

☐ Lecture (or minilectures)

☐ Drill and Recitation

☐ Computer-Assisted Instruction

☐ Independent Study

☐ Simulations

☐ Directed Reading

☐ Learning Centers

☐ Programmed Instruction

☐ Games

☐ The Project Approach

☐ Peer Tutoring

☐ Direct Instruction

☐ Discovery Learning

☐ Listening Posts

Student Name _____   Date _____

8. Regarding a possible connection between my current learning style and current teaching style, at this point I:

☐ see no relationship

☐ see one or more possible connections (please describe)

_____

_____

_____

_____

_____

_____

_____

_____

_____

_____

_____

_____

_____

_____

_____

_____

_____

_____

_____

_____

_____

_____

Student Name _____   Date _____

Journal Entry

Since this chapter focused on accepting or embracing the challenge of diversity and individual differences, your journal entry should concentrate on what you have learned about:

1. Yourself and your own potential to work with a diverse student population;

2. Your desire to modify your teaching to meet students' needs;

3. Your own thoughts and feelings about multicultural education, special education, bilingual education, and other types of supportive learning environments; and

4. Your own learning and (potential) teaching style.

_____

_____

_____

_____

_____

_____

_____

_____

_____

_____

_____

_____

_____

_____

_____

_____

Questions for Discussion

1. The authors have written:

   This commitment to diversity, which implies a pervasive and consistent attention to individual differences, is a part of the tradition, symbolic rhetoric, and legislative framework of American education; it is what makes the American classroom unique among the classrooms of the world.

   (a) Do you agree with these assertions? Why or why not?

   (b) If you don't totally agree with these assertions, to what extent do you believe they are accurate?

2. What is the relationship between special education and multicultural education? Where do these terms overlap, diverge?

3. In discussing learning-style-informed education, some practitioners have charged that it is not practical. "You just can't custom-tailor a learning environment for every learner in the class." What is your reaction to this assertion?

4. What are your thoughts about the following statement that comments on the teaching style of a multicultural educator?

   By definition, a multicultural educator's *teaching* style should be strongly influenced by the learning styles and learning needs of his or her students. She may enjoy teaching and learning in highly individualistic, competitive learning environments, love to lecture, and know and care very little about the history and demography of Mexico. *But,* if research and/or teacher experience has demonstrated that cooperative learning groups, high degrees of student active participation and discussion, and teacher knowledge of Mexican history has proven to be beneficial to the learning of her students, the multicultural educator will modify her teaching style to move in the direction of her students' learning styles and needs.

5. The material in this chapter implies that a supportive and enabling classroom teacher will be, among other things, a teacher who strives to countervail and diminish the effects of racism, sexism, elitism, handicappism, and religious intolerance in our society by positively responding to diversity and individual differences in his or her instruction.

   (a) Do you think this is an appropriate and realistic task for classroom teachers? Why? Why not?

   (b) As a future educator, how would you describe your own feelings about the various "-isms" mentioned above? Do these words, for example, represent forces that contemporary educators should be knowledgeable about, or are they artifacts of the past, deserving minimal attention?

References

Banks, J. (1987). *Teaching strategies for ethnic studies* (4th edition). Boston: Allyn and Bacon.

Bennett, C. I. (1986). *Comprehensive multicultural education: theory and practice.* Boston: Allyn and Bacon.

Chinn, P. C., & Gollnick, D. M. (1986). *Multicultural education in a pluralistic society* (2nd edition). Columbus, Ohio: Charles E. Merrill.

Davidman, L. (1984). Learning style and teaching style analysis in the teacher education curriculum: A synthesis approach. (ERIC Document Reproduction Service No. ED 249183).

Davidman, L., & Davidman, P. (1988). Multicultural teacher education in the state of California: The challenge of definition and implementation. *Teacher Education Quarterly,* 15(2), 50–67.

Sleeter, C. E., & Grant, C. A. (1988). *Making choices for multicultural education: Five approaches to race, class and gender.* Columbus, Ohio: Charles E. Merrill.

Tiedt, P. L., & Tiedt, I. M. (1986). *Multicultural teaching: A handbook of activities, information, and resources* (2nd edition). Boston: Allyn and Bacon.

Tway, E. (ed.). *Reading ladders for human relations* (6th edition). Urbana, Ill. NCTE Committee on Reading Ladders for Human Relations, National Council of Teachers of English.

C H A P T E R 1 0

On Becoming a Teacher

And, so, we will end with you. This book has been designed to be a travel book, intending to take you on a journey. Instead of purchasing an airline ticket or signing aboard for a cruise, you took a course, a course designed to introduce you to education and the world of schools. Of course, none of our readers are strangers to school, most having spent a large portion of their lives in one classroom or another. However, this journey was a "backstage tour," an opportunity to see students and schools from the other side of the footlights. If you will, through the eyes of the teachers.

You have been the reporter, the observer, the stranger in a not so strange land. You have looked at familiar objects through new lenses. You have recorded classroom behavior and tried in various ways to capture and thus better understand what goes on in schools. You have questioned children and adults about their experiences. You have seen yourself—three or 13 years earlier—in some of those students. Old memories have been provoked by the smell of the school cafeteria and the empty gymnasium. The purpose of this travel, this backstage trip through school, has not been only to gather facts, learn how to use observational instruments, or learn a few perspectives on education. Nor has it been a mere sentimental journey.

Henry David Thoreau, one of our most distinguished essayists and a crusty observer of life, once said of travel, "It is not worth while to go around the world to count the cats in Zanzibar." In other words, travel can be a potent type of educational experience; it should do something to us and for us. We should be changed as a result of the travel, seeing ourselves and our world differently as a result of observing life in Zanzibar or in P.S. 22. We will have wasted our time and money if we just collected facts or, worse, passively experienced the journey, like a film we really weren't interested in seeing or talking about. The purpose of this chapter is to help you think about your trip, putting into perspective what you have learned.

Having gained information and insights into classrooms and the people who inhabit them, we turn now to a different focus. Socrates once proclaimed that the aim of education is to "know thyself." How has your work in this course deepened your understanding of yourself? Has it clarified your understanding of what is involved in teaching? Has it given you a richer sense of what is involved? Has it helped you answer the questions, "Is teaching for me?" and "Am I for teaching?" Some of you may already have solid answers to these questions, but most of you, we suspect, will benefit from one final set of thought-provoking observation and analysis activities as you attempt to develop clearer answers to these questions. However, now, as your journey in this course is nearing completion, you will become the object of observation and analysis. And the observation activities that follow, like many others in this text, will involve you with tools that will prove valuable to you in journeys that reach far beyond this course. The self-observation, self-analysis activities that follow will lead you into a personal goal- or objective-setting activity that we hope will be the beginning of your career as an active, analytical, self-directed professional.

Core Activity
Making Yourself a Teacher

The great majority of people who teach children go through a carefully sequenced program of academic and professional courses. They are said to have gone through teacher education. They have been prepared. In one sense, this is correct. But in another, it is misleading. To go through teacher education and to be prepared is much too passive for what ought to happen.

Becoming a good teacher, like becoming a good musician or a good athlete, requires a good deal of self-initiative and self-direction. Training helps. Courses are important. Ultimately, however, the teacher makes him- or herself a good teacher. In effect, the individual is both the maker and the made; both the artist and the work of art. Such a point of view requires the maker—the future teacher—to have both the will to make the changes and the idea of what he or she is making. By "will" we mean the desire and persistence to work toward the goals of becoming a skilled and dedicated teacher. By "idea" we mean a clear vision of what is being made, a blueprint that guides your activity. For instance, if a prospective teacher discovers that he is shy, he needs to overcome this condition. He needs to put himself in situations where he is forced to reach out to others and begin to be comfortable in what is the rather public role of the teacher. Or, if a prospective teacher is a big talker, but a poor listener, she needs to learn how to limit her talking, ask more questions and carefully and patiently listen to what others are saying.

Developing the necessary will is essential, but beyond the scope of this book. However, it is our intention to assist you in developing some of the ideas that should guide your own efforts to make yourself a teacher. In order to do this, we urge you to complete three final steps.

First, reread all your answers to the exercises in this chapter with an eye toward identifying areas of strength and areas where you need to focus your attention. (If you, as yet, have not filled in all of the exercises, complete them all before going any further.)

Second, once you have made the review suggested above, list your strengths and areas needing attention in specific terms. This is an important step and you need to take time and give your full attention to it.

Areas of Strength

1. _____
2. _____
3. _____
4. _____
5. _____
6. _____
7. _____
8. _____
9. _____
10. _____
11. _____
12. _____

Areas of Needed Attention

1. _____
2. _____
3. _____
4. _____
5. _____
6. _____
7. _____
8. _____

9. _____

10. _____

11. _____

12. _____

Third, and finally, you need to develop some specific goals. Since none of us will ever be "The Perfect Teacher" and will always need to find ways to improve, we are not suggesting that you identify everything you need to reach such a never-ending goal. Rather, we want you to state in specific terms what you believe are five objectives that will bring you closer to becoming a good teacher. These five objectives should be based on the strengths, and in particular, the areas of needed attention, those unfinished parts of ourselves. They should be realistic, practical, and attainable objectives. For instance, "Making myself a great math teacher" is much too general. So, too, is "Getting over being shy." A more appropriate objective might be, "I will learn to maintain eye contact with people while speaking to them." Or, "I will learn to listen carefully to what people are saying to me."

Objective One: _____

_____

Objective Two: _____

_____

Objective Three: _____

_____

Objective Four: _____

_____

Objective Five: _____

_____

The important point, however, is that these are *your* objectives. Use them to guide your efforts at making yourself the best teacher you are capable of becoming.

Suggested Activity One

Knowing Thyself

Winston Churchill, whom many consider the greatest statesman of the twentieth century, once described Russia as an enigma wrapped in a mystery. So, too, is the self, but few of us recognize this. If we reflect on who we are for a moment, we can come up with words or ideas that describe or explain who we are. But this description or explanation is probably a superficial view of ourselves. Would our parents come up with the same description? Would our best friend or roommate see us the same way? Would a psychologist probing our unconscious confirm our own list of words and ideas?

One way to look at ourselves, to approximate who we are, is to think of certain dimensions of the self. This approach has been conceptualized in the Johari Window. The self is divided into four panes of a window, the Johari Window.

		Self	
		Things I Know	Things I Don't Know
Others	Things They Know	Arena	Blind Spot
	Things They Don't Know	Private Self	Mystery

The first window pane is called the *Arena* and represents that part of the self that is known to both ourselves and to others. It is that part of the self we present to the public that we recognize and of which we take ownership. This is familiar territory.

The second window pane (moving down) is the *Private Self.* Here is the self we typically keep secret, but might under special circumstances share with someone close to us. Often our fears and insecurities, our doubts, secret ambitions, and passions are hidden here.

The third window pane (upper right) is called the *Blind Spot.* This is the self that others see, but of which we are unaware. Contained here is a self that, if revealed to us, would surprise us. Sometimes the blind spot contains pleasant characteristics and sometimes unpleasant. It is not unlike a person with a sign pinned to the back of his or her coat that everyone but him or her can read.

The fourth window pane is called the *Mystery*. Here is the self that neither we nor the outside observers are aware of. It is completely hidden from view, but may be a strong force in our lives. It may contain dreams, passions, and fantasies of which we are not consciously aware. It is our mystery, and while we may come to know more and more of it, the mystery will never disappear (Luft, 1970).

During the next few days, complete your own Johari window. To do this, complete the following steps:

First, list five adjectives or phrases you would use to describe yourself accurately to others.

1. _____

2. _____

3. _____

4. _____

5. _____

Second, list five adjectives or phrases you feel someone else who knows you well would use to describe you.

1. _____

2. _____

3. _____

4. _____

5. _____

Third, choose a roommate or classmate who you believe knows you well and ask them to thoughtfully list five adjectives or phrases that describe you.

1. _____

2. _____

3. _____

4. _____

5. _____

Fourth, compare the lists. What have these three angles of viewing you revealed? What are the similarities in the lists? What are the differences? How do you explain the differences? What have you learned about yourself from the exercise so far?

Fifth, your instructor may or may not choose to put you in small groups to go over what you have learned in the first four steps. At this point, however, you should fill in as fully as you are able your own Johari Window.

Questions

1. What happened in this exercise that confirmed your own view of yourself? (What was not a surprise?)
2. What surprised you about yourself in doing this exercise?
3. Has your mystery window pane become smaller or larger? How? Why?

_____

_____

_____

_____

_____

_____

_____

_____

_____

_____

_____

_____

_____

_____

_____

_____

Student Name _____   Date _____

Suggested Activity Two

Your Personal Pros and Cons for Teaching

The next step in our set of self-observation activities will give you the chance, first, to compare your reasons for going into teaching with a list of reasons which in-service teachers have identified, and then to examine and comment on a set of reasons that explains why some people do not go into teaching or end their career quickly.

Directions:

1. First read each list carefully. Then, on the first column, rate the reasons in List One from 1 through 6 that together explain why you are going into teaching. Give the strongest reason a rating of 1, the next strongest a rating of 2, and so on. Then, do the same with List Two, but this time only rate the reasons that have meaning to you. Give the strongest reason a rating of 1, and so on.

List One (The Reasons Why Teachers Enter Teaching)

____ enjoy working with students

____ good fringe benefits (i.e., health insurance, long vacations, etc.)

____ doing important and honorable work

____ gives me geographic flexibility

____ chance to work with people who share my goals

____ preferable to options in the business world

____ job stability

____ doing something good for the community

____ daily/yearly schedule that gives me time to myself

____ pleasant surroundings and working conditions

List Two (The Reasons People Do Not Go into Teaching or Leave Early)

____ personally did not enjoy school and do not want to be part of it

____ looking for more material rewards from work than can be gained in teaching

____ do not want to be a disciplinarian

_____ as a teacher, not enough say in educational issues and conditions of work

_____ as a teacher, not enough opportunities for personal growth and development

_____ too much out-of-school work (i.e., preparations and paper corrections)

2. What does your set of ratings tell you about your reasons for going into teaching? Did your ratings in any way surprise you? If so, please explain why.

_____

_____

_____

_____

_____

_____

_____

3. Read the second list of reasons and comment on how you think these factors may or may not influence your decision to begin and maintain a career in teaching. Explain why these particular reasons are meaningful or not meaningful for you.

_____

_____

_____

_____

_____

_____

Suggested Activity Three

Your Ideal School

As a result of years and years of schooling, and more recently as a result of your field observations, you have developed a set of standards about schools. In fact, you have an ideal school in your mind. Much of what you think about yourself and education is wrapped up in that ideal. The following questions will help you learn about and identify factors of your ideal school. By responding to each of the questions, you will reveal dimensions of your ideal *and* of yourself.

1. What is the setting for your ideal school? Rural? Suburban? Inner city? In what part of the country or state? Be as explicit as possible.

2. What is the grade level of this school? What are the students like?

3. What is your classroom like? Physically (draw it if it helps)? Psychologically?

4. Describe the building (age, design, furnishings, outstanding features).

5. What other adults (if any) are part of your classroom?

6. What kinds of relationships exist among the faculty? Between you and your supervisor? How much supervision do you want?

7. What are some of the things you want to have happen in your ideal school?

8. What do your answers reveal about you and your career aspirations?

Suggested Activity Four
Setting Performance Priorities

"The good teacher" is a practical idea, but it is also an ideal. As elementary- and secondary-school students, we trudged off to school each September, hoping that this year would be different, that this year we would get "the good teacher," the one who would like us and teach us to like school. Sometimes we came close to the ideal, but usually not.

There is, of course, no ideal teacher. Nor is there one set of characteristics or competencies that are ideal for all teaching situations. However, there has been a substantial amount of exhortation, debate, and research in recent years in this area. The competency- or performance-based movement in teacher education, which gained momentum during the 1970s, is a result of all this ferment and has produced several useful lists of important teacher competencies. For example, as a result of an extensive study at Iowa State University, Richard Mannette (1984) and his associates came up with a thorough list of teacher competencies. These competencies, or performance areas, are based on teaching-effectiveness research as well as the practical desires of principals, school boards, and superintendents.

These competencies, or criteria as they are called in Mannette's assessment instrument, were distributed into four major performance categories: productive teaching techniques; classroom management; positive interpersonal relations; and professional responsibilities. You will recognize many of the performance areas, or competencies, listed below as the "basic stuff" of teaching, and it is almost certain that you will be evaluated in terms of *some* of these criteria if you choose to become a teacher. Therefore, it will be useful now, as you are considering your decision to become a teacher, and moving beyond that to consider a plan for personal growth in teaching, to read through the list that follows, and put a check (√) next to those performance areas in which you believe you currently possess some skill or strength and put a plus (+) next to the areas in which you believe you have a lot to learn (a high-growth area).*

In some of the performance areas, particularly those in performance area 4, you may find it difficult to rate yourself. *You do not need to put a √ or + next to each of the 26 performance areas to complete this activity.* Indeed, rating yourself in half of these performance areas will be a positive step forward toward completing the Core Activity, the most important activity in this chapter.

---

*Please note that the list employed in this text is the authors' revision of materials presented in the previously cited document co-authored by Richard Mannette.

Student Name _____ Date _____

Performance Category I
(Productive Teaching Techniques)

	Strength Area	High-Growth Area

The teacher is able to:

1. demonstrate effective lesson-planning skills

2. demonstrate effective lesson-sequence and unit-planning skills

3. effectively implement lesson plans

4. motivate students

5. effectively communicate with students

6. effectively diagnose students

7. provide students with specific evaluative feedback

8. display a thorough knowledge of subject matter

9. set appropriate expectations for student achievement

10. provide learning opportunities for individual or idiosyncratic learners

11. effectively manage classroom learning time

12. select and effectively teach content that is congruent with the prescribed curriculum

13. make effective use of time, materials, and human resources

Student Name _____   Date _____

Performance Category II	**Strength Area**	**High-Growth Area**
(Classroom Management)		

14. demonstrate evidence of personal organization   _____   _____

15. set appropriate standards for student behavior   _____   _____

16. organize students for effective instruction   _____   _____

Performance Category III
(Positive Interpersonal Relations)

17. demonstrate effective interpersonal relationships with others   _____   _____

18. demonstrate awareness of the needs of students   _____   _____

19. promote positive self-concept(s)   _____   _____

20. demonstrate sensitivity in relating to students   _____   _____

21. promote self-discipline and responsibility   _____   _____

Performance Category IV
(Professional Responsibilities)

22. demonstrate employee responsibilities   _____   _____

23. support school regulations and policies   _____   _____

24. assume responsibilities outside the classroom as they relate to school   _____   _____

25. engage in professional self-evaluation   _____   _____

26. respond positively to suggested improvements in a timely manner   _____   _____

Student Name _____   Date _____

Journal Entry

Since this is the final chapter in this workbook, and since a major objective of this workbook was to place you in a position to make a more informed choice about entering, or not entering, the teaching profession, it would be appropriate in this final journal entry to:

1. Share your decision;
2. Explain why you have made this choice; and
3. Discuss how the journey this workbook led you through contributed to your decision, *or* discuss other reasons for your decision.

_____

_____

_____

_____

_____

_____

_____

_____

_____

_____

_____

_____

_____

_____

_____

_____

_____

Questions for Discussion

1. Which two activities in this workbook/guidebook proved most illuminating for you? Why was this the case?

2. Which of your five specific objectives are you going to work on first?

3. Did the rating and self-analysis activities in this chapter lead you to specify, in your final five objectives, objectives that were a surprise to you?

4. If you had been asked to produce a set of five growth objectives at the beginning of the course, which of the final five you produced would likely *not* have been included?

References

Luft, J. (1970). *Group processes: An introduction to group dynamics* (2nd edition). Palo Alto, Calif.: National Press.

Mannette, R., & Stow, S. B. (1984). *Clinical manual for teacher performance evaluation*. Ames, Iowa: Iowa State University Foundation.

Author Index

Subject Index